C-982    CAREER EXAMINATION SERIES

*This is your*
*PASSBOOK for...*

# Police Attendant

*Test Preparation Study Guide*
*Questions & Answers*

# COPYRIGHT NOTICE

This book is SOLELY intended for, is sold ONLY to, and its use is RESTRICTED to individual, bona fide applicants or candidates who qualify by virtue of having seriously filed applications for appropriate license, certificate, professional and/or promotional advancement, higher school matriculation, scholarship, or other legitimate requirements of education and/or governmental authorities.

This book is NOT intended for use, class instruction, tutoring, training, duplication, copying, reprinting, excerption, or adaptation, etc., by:

1) Other publishers
2) Proprietors and/or Instructors of "Coaching" and/or Preparatory Courses
3) Personnel and/or Training Divisions of commercial, industrial, and governmental organizations
4) Schools, colleges, or universities and/or their departments and staffs, including teachers and other personnel
5) Testing Agencies or Bureaus
6) Study groups which seek by the purchase of a single volume to copy and/or duplicate and/or adapt this material for use by the group as a whole without having purchased individual volumes for each of the members of the group
7) Et al.

Such persons would be in violation of appropriate Federal and State statutes.

PROVISION OF LICENSING AGREEMENTS – Recognized educational, commercial, industrial, and governmental institutions and organizations, and others legitimately engaged in educational pursuits, including training, testing, and measurement activities, may address request for a licensing agreement to the copyright owners, who will determine whether, and under what conditions, including fees and charges, the materials in this book may be used them. In other words, a licensing facility exists for the legitimate use of the material in this book on other than an individual basis. However, it is asseverated and affirmed here that the material in this book CANNOT be used without the receipt of the express permission of such a licensing agreement from the Publishers. Inquiries re licensing should be addressed to the company, attention rights and permissions department.

All rights reserved, including the right of reproduction in whole or in part, in any form or by any means, electronic or mechanical, including photocopying, recording, or by any information storage and retrieval system, without permission in writing from the Publisher.

Copyright © 2024 by
## National Learning Corporation

212 Michael Drive, Syosset, NY 11791
(516) 921-8888 • www.passbooks.com
E-mail: info@passbooks.com

PUBLISHED IN THE UNITED STATES OF AMERICA

# PASSBOOK® SERIES

THE *PASSBOOK® SERIES* has been created to prepare applicants and candidates for the ultimate academic battlefield – the examination room.

At some time in our lives, each and every one of us may be required to take an examination – for validation, matriculation, admission, qualification, registration, certification, or licensure.

Based on the assumption that every applicant or candidate has met the basic formal educational standards, has taken the required number of courses, and read the necessary texts, the *PASSBOOK® SERIES* furnishes the one special preparation which may assure passing with confidence, instead of failing with insecurity. Examination questions – together with answers – are furnished as the basic vehicle for study so that the mysteries of the examination and its compounding difficulties may be eliminated or diminished by a sure method.

This book is meant to help you pass your examination provided that you qualify and are serious in your objective.

The entire field is reviewed through the huge store of content information which is succinctly presented through a provocative and challenging approach – the question-and-answer method.

A climate of success is established by furnishing the correct answers at the end of each test.

You soon learn to recognize types of questions, forms of questions, and patterns of questioning. You may even begin to anticipate expected outcomes.

You perceive that many questions are repeated or adapted so that you can gain acute insights, which may enable you to score many sure points.

You learn how to confront new questions, or types of questions, and to attack them confidently and work out the correct answers.

You note objectives and emphases, and recognize pitfalls and dangers, so that you may make positive educational adjustments.

Moreover, you are kept fully informed in relation to new concepts, methods, practices, and directions in the field.

You discover that you are actually taking the examination all the time: you are preparing for the examination by "taking" an examination, not by reading extraneous and/or supererogatory textbooks.

In short, this PASSBOOK®, used directedly, should be an important factor in helping you to pass your test.

# POLICE ATTENDANT

DUTIES AND RESPONSIBILITIES
Under direct supervision, performs guard and search duties of prisoners and detainees, and performs related work.

EXAMPLES OF TYPICAL TASKS
Searches prisoners. Fingerprints prisoners. Lodges and guards prisoners during their incarceration in cell block area. Attends to prisoners' needs such as providing food and other essentials. Inspects cells, while they are empty, for any dangerous items or contraband and informs desk officer if any such items are found. Removes dangerous items and contraband from prisoners and reports to desk officer. Maintains any records required incidental to assigned duties. Is responsible for maintaining and cleanliness of the cells.

SUBJECT OF EXAMINATION
The written test will be of the multiple-choice type and may include questions on recognizing the existence of a problem; solving problems using addition and subtraction; understanding written language; communicating information to another person; understanding the order in which to do things; applying general rules to a specific situation, or identifying a common element in several different situations; and other related areas.

# HOW TO TAKE A TEST

I. YOU MUST PASS AN EXAMINATION

A. *WHAT EVERY CANDIDATE SHOULD KNOW*

Examination applicants often ask us for help in preparing for the written test. What can I study in advance? What kinds of questions will be asked? How will the test be given? How will the papers be graded?

As an applicant for a civil service examination, you may be wondering about some of these things. Our purpose here is to suggest effective methods of advance study and to describe civil service examinations.

Your chances for success on this examination can be increased if you know how to prepare. Those "pre-examination jitters" can be reduced if you know what to expect. You can even experience an adventure in good citizenship if you know why civil service exams are given.

B. *WHY ARE CIVIL SERVICE EXAMINATIONS GIVEN?*

Civil service examinations are important to you in two ways. As a citizen, you want public jobs filled by employees who know how to do their work. As a job seeker, you want a fair chance to compete for that job on an equal footing with other candidates. The best-known means of accomplishing this two-fold goal is the competitive examination.

Exams are widely publicized throughout the nation. They may be administered for jobs in federal, state, city, municipal, town or village governments or agencies.

Any citizen may apply, with some limitations, such as the age or residence of applicants. Your experience and education may be reviewed to see whether you meet the requirements for the particular examination. When these requirements exist, they are reasonable and applied consistently to all applicants. Thus, a competitive examination may cause you some uneasiness now, but it is your privilege and safeguard.

C. *HOW ARE CIVIL SERVICE EXAMS DEVELOPED?*

Examinations are carefully written by trained technicians who are specialists in the field known as "psychological measurement," in consultation with recognized authorities in the field of work that the test will cover. These experts recommend the subject matter areas or skills to be tested; only those knowledges or skills important to your success on the job are included. The most reliable books and source materials available are used as references. Together, the experts and technicians judge the difficulty level of the questions.

Test technicians know how to phrase questions so that the problem is clearly stated. Their ethics do not permit "trick" or "catch" questions. Questions may have been tried out on sample groups, or subjected to statistical analysis, to determine their usefulness.

Written tests are often used in combination with performance tests, ratings of training and experience, and oral interviews. All of these measures combine to form the best-known means of finding the right person for the right job.

## II. HOW TO PASS THE WRITTEN TEST

### A. NATURE OF THE EXAMINATION

To prepare intelligently for civil service examinations, you should know how they differ from school examinations you have taken. In school you were assigned certain definite pages to read or subjects to cover. The examination questions were quite detailed and usually emphasized memory. Civil service exams, on the other hand, try to discover your present ability to perform the duties of a position, plus your potentiality to learn these duties. In other words, a civil service exam attempts to predict how successful you will be. Questions cover such a broad area that they cannot be as minute and detailed as school exam questions.

In the public service similar kinds of work, or positions, are grouped together in one "class." This process is known as *position-classification*. All the positions in a class are paid according to the salary range for that class. One class title covers all of these positions, and they are all tested by the same examination.

### B. FOUR BASIC STEPS

#### 1) Study the announcement

How, then, can you know what subjects to study? Our best answer is: "Learn as much as possible about the class of positions for which you've applied." The exam will test the knowledge, skills and abilities needed to do the work.

Your most valuable source of information about the position you want is the official exam announcement. This announcement lists the training and experience qualifications. Check these standards and apply only if you come reasonably close to meeting them.

The brief description of the position in the examination announcement offers some clues to the subjects which will be tested. Think about the job itself. Review the duties in your mind. Can you perform them, or are there some in which you are rusty? Fill in the blank spots in your preparation.

Many jurisdictions preview the written test in the exam announcement by including a section called "Knowledge and Abilities Required," "Scope of the Examination," or some similar heading. Here you will find out specifically what fields will be tested.

#### 2) Review your own background

Once you learn in general what the position is all about, and what you need to know to do the work, ask yourself which subjects you already know fairly well and which need improvement. You may wonder whether to concentrate on improving your strong areas or on building some background in your fields of weakness. When the announcement has specified "some knowledge" or "considerable knowledge," or has used adjectives like "beginning principles of…" or "advanced … methods," you can get a clue as to the number and difficulty of questions to be asked in any given field. More questions, and hence broader coverage, would be included for those subjects which are more important in the work. Now weigh your strengths and weaknesses against the job requirements and prepare accordingly.

#### 3) Determine the level of the position

Another way to tell how intensively you should prepare is to understand the level of the job for which you are applying. Is it the entering level? In other words, is this the position in which beginners in a field of work are hired? Or is it an intermediate or advanced level? Sometimes this is indicated by such words as "Junior" or "Senior" in the class title. Other jurisdictions use Roman numerals to designate the level – Clerk I, Clerk II, for example. The word "Supervisor" sometimes appears in the title. If the level is not indicated by the title, check the description of duties. Will you be working under very close supervision, or will you have responsibility for independent decisions in this work?

### 4) Choose appropriate study materials

Now that you know the subjects to be examined and the relative amount of each subject to be covered, you can choose suitable study materials. For beginning level jobs, or even advanced ones, if you have a pronounced weakness in some aspect of your training, read a modern, standard textbook in that field. Be sure it is up to date and has general coverage. Such books are normally available at your library, and the librarian will be glad to help you locate one. For entry-level positions, questions of appropriate difficulty are chosen – neither highly advanced questions, nor those too simple. Such questions require careful thought but not advanced training.

If the position for which you are applying is technical or advanced, you will read more advanced, specialized material. If you are already familiar with the basic principles of your field, elementary textbooks would waste your time. Concentrate on advanced textbooks and technical periodicals. Think through the concepts and review difficult problems in your field.

These are all general sources. You can get more ideas on your own initiative, following these leads. For example, training manuals and publications of the government agency which employs workers in your field can be useful, particularly for technical and professional positions. A letter or visit to the government department involved may result in more specific study suggestions, and certainly will provide you with a more definite idea of the exact nature of the position you are seeking.

## III. KINDS OF TESTS

Tests are used for purposes other than measuring knowledge and ability to perform specified duties. For some positions, it is equally important to test ability to make adjustments to new situations or to profit from training. In others, basic mental abilities not dependent on information are essential. Questions which test these things may not appear as pertinent to the duties of the position as those which test for knowledge and information. Yet they are often highly important parts of a fair examination. For very general questions, it is almost impossible to help you direct your study efforts. What we can do is to point out some of the more common of these general abilities needed in public service positions and describe some typical questions.

1) General information

Broad, general information has been found useful for predicting job success in some kinds of work. This is tested in a variety of ways, from vocabulary lists to questions about current events. Basic background in some field of work, such as sociology or economics, may be sampled in a group of questions. Often these are principles which have become familiar to most persons through exposure rather than through formal training. It is difficult to advise you how to study for these questions; being alert to the world around you is our best suggestion.

2) Verbal ability

An example of an ability needed in many positions is verbal or language ability. Verbal ability is, in brief, the ability to use and understand words. Vocabulary and grammar tests are typical measures of this ability. Reading comprehension or paragraph interpretation questions are common in many kinds of civil service tests. You are given a paragraph of written material and asked to find its central meaning.

### 3) Numerical ability

Number skills can be tested by the familiar arithmetic problem, by checking paired lists of numbers to see which are alike and which are different, or by interpreting charts and graphs. In the latter test, a graph may be printed in the test booklet which you are asked to use as the basis for answering questions.

### 4) Observation

A popular test for law-enforcement positions is the observation test. A picture is shown to you for several minutes, then taken away. Questions about the picture test your ability to observe both details and larger elements.

### 5) Following directions

In many positions in the public service, the employee must be able to carry out written instructions dependably and accurately. You may be given a chart with several columns, each column listing a variety of information. The questions require you to carry out directions involving the information given in the chart.

### 6) Skills and aptitudes

Performance tests effectively measure some manual skills and aptitudes. When the skill is one in which you are trained, such as typing or shorthand, you can practice. These tests are often very much like those given in business school or high school courses. For many of the other skills and aptitudes, however, no short-time preparation can be made. Skills and abilities natural to you or that you have developed throughout your lifetime are being tested.

Many of the general questions just described provide all the data needed to answer the questions and ask you to use your reasoning ability to find the answers. Your best preparation for these tests, as well as for tests of facts and ideas, is to be at your physical and mental best. You, no doubt, have your own methods of getting into an exam-taking mood and keeping "in shape." The next section lists some ideas on this subject.

## IV. KINDS OF QUESTIONS

Only rarely is the "essay" question, which you answer in narrative form, used in civil service tests. Civil service tests are usually of the short-answer type. Full instructions for answering these questions will be given to you at the examination. But in case this is your first experience with short-answer questions and separate answer sheets, here is what you need to know:

### 1) Multiple-choice Questions

Most popular of the short-answer questions is the "multiple choice" or "best answer" question. It can be used, for example, to test for factual knowledge, ability to solve problems or judgment in meeting situations found at work.

A multiple-choice question is normally one of three types—

- It can begin with an incomplete statement followed by several possible endings. You are to find the one ending which *best* completes the statement, although some of the others may not be entirely wrong.
- It can also be a complete statement in the form of a question which is answered by choosing one of the statements listed.

- It can be in the form of a problem – again you select the best answer.

Here is an example of a multiple-choice question with a discussion which should give you some clues as to the method for choosing the right answer:

When an employee has a complaint about his assignment, the action which will *best* help him overcome his difficulty is to
    A. discuss his difficulty with his coworkers
    B. take the problem to the head of the organization
    C. take the problem to the person who gave him the assignment
    D. say nothing to anyone about his complaint

In answering this question, you should study each of the choices to find which is best. Consider choice "A" – Certainly an employee may discuss his complaint with fellow employees, but no change or improvement can result, and the complaint remains unresolved. Choice "B" is a poor choice since the head of the organization probably does not know what assignment you have been given, and taking your problem to him is known as "going over the head" of the supervisor. The supervisor, or person who made the assignment, is the person who can clarify it or correct any injustice. Choice "C" is, therefore, correct. To say nothing, as in choice "D," is unwise. Supervisors have and interest in knowing the problems employees are facing, and the employee is seeking a solution to his problem.

## 2) True/False Questions

The "true/false" or "right/wrong" form of question is sometimes used. Here a complete statement is given. Your job is to decide whether the statement is right or wrong.

SAMPLE: A roaming cell-phone call to a nearby city costs less than a non-roaming call to a distant city.

This statement is wrong, or false, since roaming calls are more expensive.

This is not a complete list of all possible question forms, although most of the others are variations of these common types. You will always get complete directions for answering questions. Be sure you understand *how* to mark your answers – ask questions until you do.


## V. RECORDING YOUR ANSWERS

Computer terminals are used more and more today for many different kinds of exams.
For an examination with very few applicants, you may be told to record your answers in the test booklet itself. Separate answer sheets are much more common. If this separate answer sheet is to be scored by machine – and this is often the case – it is highly important that you mark your answers correctly in order to get credit.
An electronic scoring machine is often used in civil service offices because of the speed with which papers can be scored. Machine-scored answer sheets must be marked with a pencil, which will be given to you. This pencil has a high graphite content which responds to the electronic scoring machine. As a matter of fact, stray dots may register as answers, so do not let your pencil rest on the answer sheet while you are pondering the correct answer. Also, if your pencil lead breaks or is otherwise defective, ask for another.

Since the answer sheet will be dropped in a slot in the scoring machine, be careful not to bend the corners or get the paper crumpled.

The answer sheet normally has five vertical columns of numbers, with 30 numbers to a column. These numbers correspond to the question numbers in your test booklet. After each number, going across the page are four or five pairs of dotted lines. These short dotted lines have small letters or numbers above them. The first two pairs may also have a "T" or "F" above the letters. This indicates that the first two pairs only are to be used if the questions are of the true-false type. If the questions are multiple choice, disregard the "T" and "F" and pay attention only to the small letters or numbers.

Answer your questions in the manner of the sample that follows:

32. The largest city in the United States is
    A. Washington, D.C.
    B. New York City
    C. Chicago
    D. Detroit
    E. San Francisco

1) Choose the answer you think is best. (New York City is the largest, so "B" is correct.)
2) Find the row of dotted lines numbered the same as the question you are answering. (Find row number 32)
3) Find the pair of dotted lines corresponding to the answer. (Find the pair of lines under the mark "B.")
4) Make a solid black mark between the dotted lines.

## VI. BEFORE THE TEST

Common sense will help you find procedures to follow to get ready for an examination. Too many of us, however, overlook these sensible measures. Indeed, nervousness and fatigue have been found to be the most serious reasons why applicants fail to do their best on civil service tests. Here is a list of reminders:

- Begin your preparation early – Don't wait until the last minute to go scurrying around for books and materials or to find out what the position is all about.
- Prepare continuously – An hour a night for a week is better than an all-night cram session. This has been definitely established. What is more, a night a week for a month will return better dividends than crowding your study into a shorter period of time.
- Locate the place of the exam – You have been sent a notice telling you when and where to report for the examination. If the location is in a different town or otherwise unfamiliar to you, it would be well to inquire the best route and learn something about the building.
- Relax the night before the test – Allow your mind to rest. Do not study at all that night. Plan some mild recreation or diversion; then go to bed early and get a good night's sleep.
- Get up early enough to make a leisurely trip to the place for the test – This way unforeseen events, traffic snarls, unfamiliar buildings, etc. will not upset you.
- Dress comfortably – A written test is not a fashion show. You will be known by number and not by name, so wear something comfortable.

- Leave excess paraphernalia at home – Shopping bags and odd bundles will get in your way. You need bring only the items mentioned in the official notice you received; usually everything you need is provided. Do not bring reference books to the exam. They will only confuse those last minutes and be taken away from you when in the test room.
- Arrive somewhat ahead of time – If because of transportation schedules you must get there very early, bring a newspaper or magazine to take your mind off yourself while waiting.
- Locate the examination room – When you have found the proper room, you will be directed to the seat or part of the room where you will sit. Sometimes you are given a sheet of instructions to read while you are waiting. Do not fill out any forms until you are told to do so; just read them and be prepared.
- Relax and prepare to listen to the instructions
- If you have any physical problem that may keep you from doing your best, be sure to tell the test administrator. If you are sick or in poor health, you really cannot do your best on the exam. You can come back and take the test some other time.

## VII. AT THE TEST

The day of the test is here and you have the test booklet in your hand. The temptation to get going is very strong. Caution! There is more to success than knowing the right answers. You must know how to identify your papers and understand variations in the type of short-answer question used in this particular examination. Follow these suggestions for maximum results from your efforts:

### 1) Cooperate with the monitor

The test administrator has a duty to create a situation in which you can be as much at ease as possible. He will give instructions, tell you when to begin, check to see that you are marking your answer sheet correctly, and so on. He is not there to guard you, although he will see that your competitors do not take unfair advantage. He wants to help you do your best.

### 2) Listen to all instructions

Don't jump the gun! Wait until you understand all directions. In most civil service tests you get more time than you need to answer the questions. So don't be in a hurry. Read each word of instructions until you clearly understand the meaning. Study the examples, listen to all announcements and follow directions. Ask questions if you do not understand what to do.

### 3) Identify your papers

Civil service exams are usually identified by number only. You will be assigned a number; you must not put your name on your test papers. Be sure to copy your number correctly. Since more than one exam may be given, copy your exact examination title.

### 4) Plan your time

Unless you are told that a test is a "speed" or "rate of work" test, speed itself is usually not important. Time enough to answer all the questions will be provided, but this does not mean that you have all day. An overall time limit has been set. Divide the total time (in minutes) by the number of questions to determine the approximate time you have for each question.

**5) Do not linger over difficult questions**

If you come across a difficult question, mark it with a paper clip (useful to have along) and come back to it when you have been through the booklet. One caution if you do this – be sure to skip a number on your answer sheet as well. Check often to be sure that you have not lost your place and that you are marking in the row numbered the same as the question you are answering.

**6) Read the questions**

Be sure you know what the question asks! Many capable people are unsuccessful because they failed to *read* the questions correctly.

**7) Answer all questions**

Unless you have been instructed that a penalty will be deducted for incorrect answers, it is better to guess than to omit a question.

**8) Speed tests**

It is often better NOT to guess on speed tests. It has been found that on timed tests people are tempted to spend the last few seconds before time is called in marking answers at random – without even reading them – in the hope of picking up a few extra points. To discourage this practice, the instructions may warn you that your score will be "corrected" for guessing. That is, a penalty will be applied. The incorrect answers will be deducted from the correct ones, or some other penalty formula will be used.

**9) Review your answers**

If you finish before time is called, go back to the questions you guessed or omitted to give them further thought. Review other answers if you have time.

**10) Return your test materials**

If you are ready to leave before others have finished or time is called, take ALL your materials to the monitor and leave quietly. Never take any test material with you. The monitor can discover whose papers are not complete, and taking a test booklet may be grounds for disqualification.

## VIII. EXAMINATION TECHNIQUES

1) Read the general instructions carefully. These are usually printed on the first page of the exam booklet. As a rule, these instructions refer to the timing of the examination; the fact that you should not start work until the signal and must stop work at a signal, etc. If there are any *special* instructions, such as a choice of questions to be answered, make sure that you note this instruction carefully.

2) When you are ready to start work on the examination, that is as soon as the signal has been given, read the instructions to each question booklet, underline any key words or phrases, such as *least, best, outline, describe* and the like. In this way you will tend to answer as requested rather than discover on reviewing your paper that you *listed without describing*, that you selected the *worst* choice rather than the *best* choice, etc.

3) If the examination is of the objective or multiple-choice type – that is, each question will also give a series of possible answers: A, B, C or D, and you are called upon to select the best answer and write the letter next to that answer on your answer paper – it is advisable to start answering each question in turn. There may be anywhere from 50 to 100 such questions in the three or four hours allotted and you can see how much time would be taken if you read through all the questions before beginning to answer any. Furthermore, if you come across a question or group of questions which you know would be difficult to answer, it would undoubtedly affect your handling of all the other questions.

4) If the examination is of the essay type and contains but a few questions, it is a moot point as to whether you should read all the questions before starting to answer any one. Of course, if you are given a choice – say five out of seven and the like – then it is essential to read all the questions so you can eliminate the two that are most difficult. If, however, you are asked to answer all the questions, there may be danger in trying to answer the easiest one first because you may find that you will spend too much time on it. The best technique is to answer the first question, then proceed to the second, etc.

5) Time your answers. Before the exam begins, write down the time it started, then add the time allowed for the examination and write down the time it must be completed, then divide the time available somewhat as follows:
    - If 3-1/2 hours are allowed, that would be 210 minutes. If you have 80 objective-type questions, that would be an average of 2-1/2 minutes per question. Allow yourself no more than 2 minutes per question, or a total of 160 minutes, which will permit about 50 minutes to review.
    - If for the time allotment of 210 minutes there are 7 essay questions to answer, that would average about 30 minutes a question. Give yourself only 25 minutes per question so that you have about 35 minutes to review.

6) The most important instruction is to *read each question* and make sure you know what is wanted. The second most important instruction is to *time yourself properly* so that you answer every question. The third most important instruction is to *answer every question*. Guess if you have to but include something for each question. Remember that you will receive no credit for a blank and will probably receive some credit if you write something in answer to an essay question. If you guess a letter – say "B" for a multiple-choice question – you may have guessed right. If you leave a blank as an answer to a multiple-choice question, the examiners may respect your feelings but it will not add a point to your score. Some exams may penalize you for wrong answers, so in such cases *only*, you may not want to guess unless you have some basis for your answer.

7) Suggestions
    a. Objective-type questions
        1. Examine the question booklet for proper sequence of pages and questions
        2. Read all instructions carefully
        3. Skip any question which seems too difficult; return to it after all other questions have been answered
        4. Apportion your time properly; do not spend too much time on any single question or group of questions

5. Note and underline key words – *all, most, fewest, least, best, worst, same, opposite,* etc.
6. Pay particular attention to negatives
7. Note unusual option, e.g., unduly long, short, complex, different or similar in content to the body of the question
8. Observe the use of "hedging" words – *probably, may, most likely,* etc.
9. Make sure that your answer is put next to the same number as the question
10. Do not second-guess unless you have good reason to believe the second answer is definitely more correct
11. Cross out original answer if you decide another answer is more accurate; do not erase until you are ready to hand your paper in
12. Answer all questions; guess unless instructed otherwise
13. Leave time for review

b. Essay questions
1. Read each question carefully
2. Determine exactly what is wanted. Underline key words or phrases.
3. Decide on outline or paragraph answer
4. Include many different points and elements unless asked to develop any one or two points or elements
5. Show impartiality by giving pros and cons unless directed to select one side only
6. Make and write down any assumptions you find necessary to answer the questions
7. Watch your English, grammar, punctuation and choice of words
8. Time your answers; don't crowd material

8) Answering the essay question

Most essay questions can be answered by framing the specific response around several key words or ideas. Here are a few such key words or ideas:

M's: manpower, materials, methods, money, management
P's: purpose, program, policy, plan, procedure, practice, problems, pitfalls, personnel, public relations

   a. Six basic steps in handling problems:
      1. Preliminary plan and background development
      2. Collect information, data and facts
      3. Analyze and interpret information, data and facts
      4. Analyze and develop solutions as well as make recommendations
      5. Prepare report and sell recommendations
      6. Install recommendations and follow up effectiveness

   b. Pitfalls to avoid
      1. *Taking things for granted* – A statement of the situation does not necessarily imply that each of the elements is necessarily true; for example, a complaint may be invalid and biased so that all that can be taken for granted is that a complaint has been registered

2. *Considering only one side of a situation* – Wherever possible, indicate several alternatives and then point out the reasons you selected the best one
3. *Failing to indicate follow up* – Whenever your answer indicates action on your part, make certain that you will take proper follow-up action to see how successful your recommendations, procedures or actions turn out to be
4. *Taking too long in answering any single question* – Remember to time your answers properly

## IX. AFTER THE TEST

Scoring procedures differ in detail among civil service jurisdictions although the general principles are the same. Whether the papers are hand-scored or graded by machine we have described, they are nearly always graded by number. That is, the person who marks the paper knows only the number – never the name – of the applicant. Not until all the papers have been graded will they be matched with names. If other tests, such as training and experience or oral interview ratings have been given, scores will be combined. Different parts of the examination usually have different weights. For example, the written test might count 60 percent of the final grade, and a rating of training and experience 40 percent. In many jurisdictions, veterans will have a certain number of points added to their grades.

After the final grade has been determined, the names are placed in grade order and an eligible list is established. There are various methods for resolving ties between those who get the same final grade – probably the most common is to place first the name of the person whose application was received first. Job offers are made from the eligible list in the order the names appear on it. You will be notified of your grade and your rank as soon as all these computations have been made. This will be done as rapidly as possible.

People who are found to meet the requirements in the announcement are called "eligibles." Their names are put on a list of eligible candidates. An eligible's chances of getting a job depend on how high he stands on this list and how fast agencies are filling jobs from the list.

When a job is to be filled from a list of eligibles, the agency asks for the names of people on the list of eligibles for that job. When the civil service commission receives this request, it sends to the agency the names of the three people highest on this list. Or, if the job to be filled has specialized requirements, the office sends the agency the names of the top three persons who meet these requirements from the general list.

The appointing officer makes a choice from among the three people whose names were sent to him. If the selected person accepts the appointment, the names of the others are put back on the list to be considered for future openings.

That is the rule in hiring from all kinds of eligible lists, whether they are for typist, carpenter, chemist, or something else. For every vacancy, the appointing officer has his choice of any one of the top three eligibles on the list. This explains why the person whose name is on top of the list sometimes does not get an appointment when some of the persons lower on the list do. If the appointing officer chooses the second or third eligible, the No. 1 eligible does not get a job at once, but stays on the list until he is appointed or the list is terminated.

## X. HOW TO PASS THE INTERVIEW TEST

The examination for which you applied requires an oral interview test. You have already taken the written test and you are now being called for the interview test – the final part of the formal examination.

You may think that it is not possible to prepare for an interview test and that there are no procedures to follow during an interview. Our purpose is to point out some things you can do in advance that will help you and some good rules to follow and pitfalls to avoid while you are being interviewed.

*What is an interview supposed to test?*

The written examination is designed to test the technical knowledge and competence of the candidate; the oral is designed to evaluate intangible qualities, not readily measured otherwise, and to establish a list showing the relative fitness of each candidate – as measured against his competitors – for the position sought. Scoring is not on the basis of "right" and "wrong," but on a sliding scale of values ranging from "not passable" to "outstanding." As a matter of fact, it is possible to achieve a relatively low score without a single "incorrect" answer because of evident weakness in the qualities being measured.

Occasionally, an examination may consist entirely of an oral test – either an individual or a group oral. In such cases, information is sought concerning the technical knowledges and abilities of the candidate, since there has been no written examination for this purpose. More commonly, however, an oral test is used to supplement a written examination.

*Who conducts interviews?*

The composition of oral boards varies among different jurisdictions. In nearly all, a representative of the personnel department serves as chairman. One of the members of the board may be a representative of the department in which the candidate would work. In some cases, "outside experts" are used, and, frequently, a businessman or some other representative of the general public is asked to serve. Labor and management or other special groups may be represented. The aim is to secure the services of experts in the appropriate field.

However the board is composed, it is a good idea (and not at all improper or unethical) to ascertain in advance of the interview who the members are and what groups they represent. When you are introduced to them, you will have some idea of their backgrounds and interests, and at least you will not stutter and stammer over their names.

*What should be done before the interview?*

While knowledge about the board members is useful and takes some of the surprise element out of the interview, there is other preparation which is more substantive. It *is* possible to prepare for an oral interview – in several ways:

**1) Keep a copy of your application and review it carefully before the interview**

This may be the only document before the oral board, and the starting point of the interview. Know what education and experience you have listed there, and the sequence and dates of all of it. Sometimes the board will ask you to review the highlights of your experience for them; you should not have to hem and haw doing it.

**2) Study the class specification and the examination announcement**

Usually, the oral board has one or both of these to guide them. The qualities, characteristics or knowledges required by the position sought are stated in these documents. They offer valuable clues as to the nature of the oral interview. For example, if the job involves supervisory responsibilities, the announcement will usually indicate that knowledge of modern supervisory methods and the qualifications of the candidate as a supervisor will be tested. If so, you can expect such questions, frequently in the form of a hypothetical situation which you are expected to solve. NEVER go into an oral without knowledge of the duties and responsibilities of the job you seek.

### 3) Think through each qualification required

Try to visualize the kind of questions you would ask if you were a board member. How well could you answer them? Try especially to appraise your own knowledge and background in each area, *measured against the job sought*, and identify any areas in which you are weak. Be critical and realistic – do not flatter yourself.

### 4) Do some general reading in areas in which you feel you may be weak

For example, if the job involves supervision and your past experience has NOT, some general reading in supervisory methods and practices, particularly in the field of human relations, might be useful. Do NOT study agency procedures or detailed manuals. The oral board will be testing your understanding and capacity, not your memory.

### 5) Get a good night's sleep and watch your general health and mental attitude

You will want a clear head at the interview. Take care of a cold or any other minor ailment, and of course, no hangovers.

*What should be done on the day of the interview?*

Now comes the day of the interview itself. Give yourself plenty of time to get there. Plan to arrive somewhat ahead of the scheduled time, particularly if your appointment is in the fore part of the day. If a previous candidate fails to appear, the board might be ready for you a bit early. By early afternoon an oral board is almost invariably behind schedule if there are many candidates, and you may have to wait. Take along a book or magazine to read, or your application to review, but leave any extraneous material in the waiting room when you go in for your interview. In any event, relax and compose yourself.

The matter of dress is important. The board is forming impressions about you – from your experience, your manners, your attitude, and your appearance. Give your personal appearance careful attention. Dress your best, but not your flashiest. Choose conservative, appropriate clothing, and be sure it is immaculate. This is a business interview, and your appearance should indicate that you regard it as such. Besides, being well groomed and properly dressed will help boost your confidence.

Sooner or later, someone will call your name and escort you into the interview room. *This is it.* From here on you are on your own. It is too late for any more preparation. But remember, you asked for this opportunity to prove your fitness, and you are here because your request was granted.

*What happens when you go in?*

The usual sequence of events will be as follows: The clerk (who is often the board stenographer) will introduce you to the chairman of the oral board, who will introduce you to the other members of the board. Acknowledge the introductions before you sit down. Do not be surprised if you find a microphone facing you or a stenotypist sitting by. Oral interviews are usually recorded in the event of an appeal or other review.

Usually the chairman of the board will open the interview by reviewing the highlights of your education and work experience from your application – primarily for the benefit of the other members of the board, as well as to get the material into the record. Do not interrupt or comment unless there is an error or significant misinterpretation; if that is the case, do not hesitate. But do not quibble about insignificant matters. Also, he will usually ask you some question about your education, experience or your present job – partly to get you to start talking and to establish the interviewing "rapport." He may start the actual questioning, or turn it over to one of the other members. Frequently, each member undertakes the questioning on a particular area, one in which he is perhaps most competent, so you can expect each member to participate in the examination. Because time is limited, you may also expect some rather abrupt switches in the direction the questioning takes, so do not be upset by it. Normally, a board member will not pursue a single line of questioning unless he discovers a particular strength or weakness.

After each member has participated, the chairman will usually ask whether any member has any further questions, then will ask you if you have anything you wish to add. Unless you are expecting this question, it may floor you. Worse, it may start you off on an extended, extemporaneous speech. The board is not usually seeking more information. The question is principally to offer you a last opportunity to present further qualifications or to indicate that you have nothing to add. So, if you feel that a significant qualification or characteristic has been overlooked, it is proper to point it out in a sentence or so. Do not compliment the board on the thoroughness of their examination – they have been sketchy, and you know it. If you wish, merely say, "No thank you, I have nothing further to add." This is a point where you can "talk yourself out" of a good impression or fail to present an important bit of information. Remember, *you close the interview yourself*.

The chairman will then say, "That is all, Mr. _____, thank you." Do not be startled; the interview is over, and quicker than you think. Thank him, gather your belongings and take your leave. Save your sigh of relief for the other side of the door.

*How to put your best foot forward*

Throughout this entire process, you may feel that the board individually and collectively is trying to pierce your defenses, seek out your hidden weaknesses and embarrass and confuse you. Actually, this is not true. They are obliged to make an appraisal of your qualifications for the job you are seeking, and they want to see you in your best light. Remember, they must interview all candidates and a non-cooperative candidate may become a failure in spite of their best efforts to bring out his qualifications. Here are 15 suggestions that will help you:

**1) Be natural – Keep your attitude confident, not cocky**

If you are not confident that you can do the job, do not expect the board to be. Do not apologize for your weaknesses, try to bring out your strong points. The board is interested in a positive, not negative, presentation. Cockiness will antagonize any board member and make him wonder if you are covering up a weakness by a false show of strength.

**2) Get comfortable, but don't lounge or sprawl**

Sit erectly but not stiffly. A careless posture may lead the board to conclude that you are careless in other things, or at least that you are not impressed by the importance of the occasion. Either conclusion is natural, even if incorrect. Do not fuss with your clothing, a pencil or an ashtray. Your hands may occasionally be useful to emphasize a point; do not let them become a point of distraction.

**3) Do not wisecrack or make small talk**

This is a serious situation, and your attitude should show that you consider it as such. Further, the time of the board is limited – they do not want to waste it, and neither should you.

### 4) Do not exaggerate your experience or abilities

In the first place, from information in the application or other interviews and sources, the board may know more about you than you think. Secondly, you probably will not get away with it. An experienced board is rather adept at spotting such a situation, so do not take the chance.

### 5) If you know a board member, do not make a point of it, yet do not hide it

Certainly you are not fooling him, and probably not the other members of the board. Do not try to take advantage of your acquaintanceship – it will probably do you little good.

### 6) Do not dominate the interview

Let the board do that. They will give you the clues – do not assume that you have to do all the talking. Realize that the board has a number of questions to ask you, and do not try to take up all the interview time by showing off your extensive knowledge of the answer to the first one.

### 7) Be attentive

You only have 20 minutes or so, and you should keep your attention at its sharpest throughout. When a member is addressing a problem or question to you, give him your undivided attention. Address your reply principally to him, but do not exclude the other board members.

### 8) Do not interrupt

A board member may be stating a problem for you to analyze. He will ask you a question when the time comes. Let him state the problem, and wait for the question.

### 9) Make sure you understand the question

Do not try to answer until you are sure what the question is. If it is not clear, restate it in your own words or ask the board member to clarify it for you. However, do not haggle about minor elements.

### 10) Reply promptly but not hastily

A common entry on oral board rating sheets is "candidate responded readily," or "candidate hesitated in replies." Respond as promptly and quickly as you can, but do not jump to a hasty, ill-considered answer.

### 11) Do not be peremptory in your answers

A brief answer is proper – but do not fire your answer back. That is a losing game from your point of view. The board member can probably ask questions much faster than you can answer them.

### 12) Do not try to create the answer you think the board member wants

He is interested in what kind of mind you have and how it works – not in playing games. Furthermore, he can usually spot this practice and will actually grade you down on it.

### 13) Do not switch sides in your reply merely to agree with a board member

Frequently, a member will take a contrary position merely to draw you out and to see if you are willing and able to defend your point of view. Do not start a debate, yet do not surrender a good position. If a position is worth taking, it is worth defending.

### 14) Do not be afraid to admit an error in judgment if you are shown to be wrong

The board knows that you are forced to reply without any opportunity for careful consideration. Your answer may be demonstrably wrong. If so, admit it and get on with the interview.

### 15) Do not dwell at length on your present job

The opening question may relate to your present assignment. Answer the question but do not go into an extended discussion. You are being examined for a *new* job, not your present one. As a matter of fact, try to phrase ALL your answers in terms of the job for which you are being examined.

*Basis of Rating*

Probably you will forget most of these "do's" and "don'ts" when you walk into the oral interview room. Even remembering them all will not ensure you a passing grade. Perhaps you did not have the qualifications in the first place. But remembering them will help you to put your best foot forward, without treading on the toes of the board members.

Rumor and popular opinion to the contrary notwithstanding, an oral board wants you to make the best appearance possible. They know you are under pressure – but they also want to see how you respond to it as a guide to what your reaction would be under the pressures of the job you seek. They will be influenced by the degree of poise you display, the personal traits you show and the manner in which you respond.


ABOUT THIS BOOK

This book contains tests divided into Examination Sections. Go through each test, answering every question in the margin. We have also attached a sample answer sheet at the back of the book that can be removed and used. At the end of each test look at the answer key and check your answers. On the ones you got wrong, look at the right answer choice and learn. Do not fill in the answers first. Do not memorize the questions and answers, but understand the answer and principles involved. On your test, the questions will likely be different from the samples. Questions are changed and new ones added. If you understand these past questions you should have success with any changes that arise. Tests may consist of several types of questions. We have additional books on each subject should more study be advisable or necessary for you. Finally, the more you study, the better prepared you will be. This book is intended to be the last thing you study before you walk into the examination room. Prior study of relevant texts is also recommended. NLC publishes some of these in our Fundamental Series. Knowledge and good sense are important factors in passing your exam. Good luck also helps. So now study this Passbook, absorb the material contained within and take that knowledge into the examination. Then do your best to pass that exam.

# EXAMINATION SECTION

# EXAMINATION SECTION
## TEST 1

DIRECTIONS: Each question or incomplete statement is followed by several suggested answers or completions. Select the one that BEST answers the question or completes the statement. *PRINT THE LETTER OF THE CORRECT ANSWER IN THE SPACE AT THE RIGHT.*

Questions 1-6.

DIRECTIONS: Questions 1 through 6 are to be answered on the basis of the following list of items permitted in cells.

| ITEMS PERMITTED IN CELLS | |
|---|---|
| comb | mop |
| spoon | towel |
| cup | letters |
| envelopes | pen |
| broom | soap |
| washcloth | money |
| writing paper | chair |
| books | dustpan |
| toothpaste | brushes |
| toothbrush | pencil |

The questions consist of sets of pictures of four objects labeled A, B, C, and D. Choose the one object that is NOT in the above list of items permitted and mark its letter in the space at the right. Disregard any information you may have about what is or is not permitted in any institution. Base your answers SOLELY on the above list. Mark only one answer for each question.

1.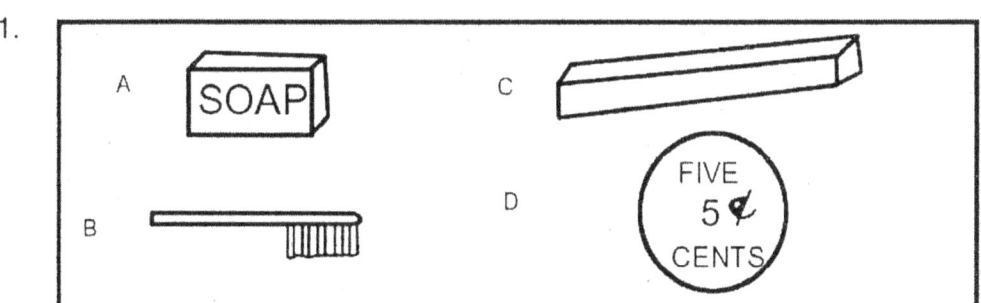

1.____

2.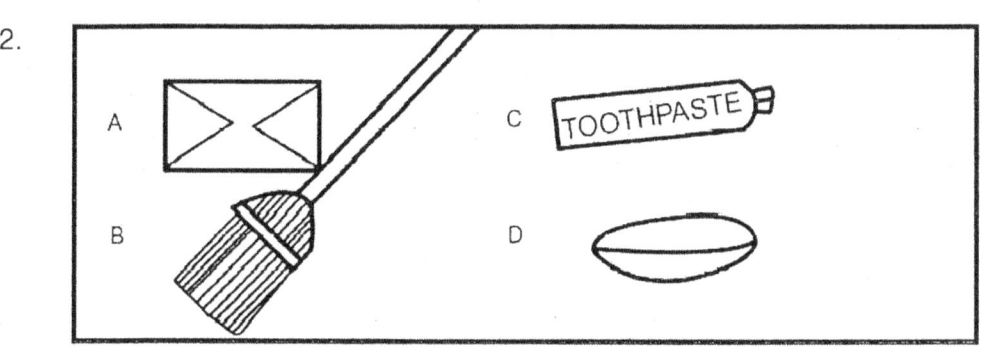

2.____

1

2 (#1)

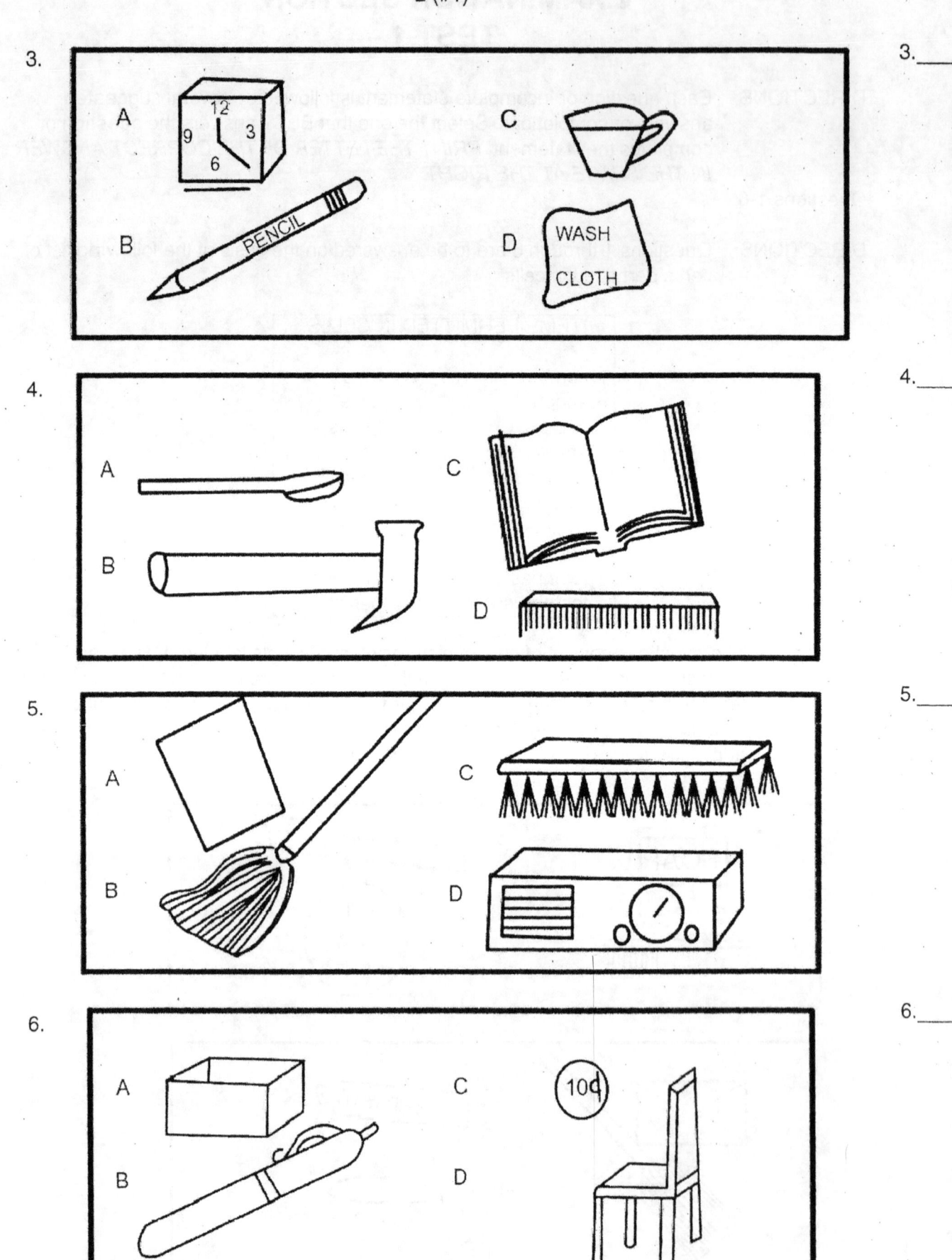

Questions 7-11.

DIRECTIONS: Questions 7 through 11 are to be answered on the basis of the following list showing the name and number of each of nine inmates.

| 1 | - Johnson | 4 | - Thompson | 7 | - Gordon |
| 2 | - Smith | 5 | - Frank | 8 | - Porter |
| 3 | - Edwards | 6 | - Murray | 9 | - Lopez |

Each question consists of 3 sets of numbers and letters.
Each set should consist of the numbers of three inmates and the first letter of each of their names. The letters should be in the same order as the numbers. In at least two of the three choices, there will be an error.

In the space at the right, mark only that choice in which the letters correspond with the numbers and are in the same order. If all three sets are wrong, mark Choice D in the space at the right.

SAMPLE QUESTION: A. 386 EPM
B. 542 FST
C. 474 LGT

Since 3 corresponds to E for Edwards, 8 corresponds to P for Porter, and 6 corresponds to M for Murray, Choice A is correct and should be entered in the answer space. Choice B is wrong because letters T and S have been reversed. Choice C is wrong because the first number, which is 4, does NOT correspond with the first letter of Choice C, which is L. It should have been T. If Choice A were also wrong, then D would have been the correct answer.

7. A. 382 EGS  B. 461 TMJ  C. 875 PLF  7.____

8. A. 549 FLT  B. 692 MJS  C. 758 GSP  8.____

9. A. 936 LEM  B. 253 FSE  C. 147 JTL  9.____

10. A. 569 PML  B. 716 GJP  C. 842 PTS  10.____

11. A. 356 FEM  B. 198 JPL  C. 637 MEG  11.____

Questions 12-16.

DIRECTIONS: Questions 12 through 16 are to be answered on the basis of the following passage.

*Mental disorders are found in a fairly large number of the inmates in correctional institutions. There are no exact figures as to the number of inmates who are mentally disturbed — partly because it is hard to draw a precise line between "mental disturbance" and "normality" — but experts find that somewhere between 15% and 25% of inmates are suffering from disorders that are obvious enough to show up in routine psychiatric examinations. Society has not yet really come to grips with the problem of what to do with mentally disturbed offenders. There is not enough money available to set up treatment programs for all the people identified as mentally disturbed; and there would probably not be enough qualified psychiatric personnel available to run such programs even if they could be set up. Most mentally disturbed offenders are therefore left to serve out their time in correctional institutions, and the burden of dealing with them falls on correction officers. This means that a correction officer must be sensitive enough to human behavior to know when he is dealing with a person who is not mentally normal, and that the officer must be imaginative enough to be able to sense how an abnormal individual might react under certain circumstances.*

12. According to the above passage, mentally disturbed inmates in correctional institutions    12.____

    A. are usually transferred to mental hospitals when their condition is noticed
    B. cannot be told from other inmates because tests cannot distinguish between insane people and normal people
    C. may constitute as much as 25% of the total inmate population
    D. should be regarded as no different from all the other inmates

13. The above passage says that today the job of handling mentally disturbed inmates is MAINLY up to    13.____

    A. psychiatric personnel        B. other inmates
    C. correction officers          D. administrative officials

14. Of the following, which is a reason given in the above passage for society's failure to provide adequate treatment programs for mentally disturbed inmates?    14.____

    A. Law-abiding citizens should not have to pay for fancy treatment programs for citizens.
    B. A person who breaks the law should not expect society to give him special help.
    C. It is impossible to tell whether an inmate is mentally disturbed.
    D. There are not enough trained people to provide the kind of treatment needed.

15. The expression *abnormal individual,* as used in the last sentence of the above passage, refers to an individual who is    15.____

    A. of average intelligence      B. of superior intelligence
    C. completely normal            D. mentally disturbed

16. The reader of the above passage would MOST likely agree that    16.____

    A. correction officers should not expect mentally disturbed persons to behave the same way a normal person would behave
    B. correction officers should not report infractions
    C. of the rules committed by mentally disturbed persons
    D. mentally disturbed persons who break the law should be treated exactly the same way as anyone else
    E. mentally disturbed persons who have broken the law should not be imprisoned

Questions 17-23.

DIRECTIONS: Questions 17 through 23 are to be answered on the basis of the roster of inmates, the instructions, the table, and the sample question given below.

*Twelve inmates of a correctional institution are divided into three permanent groups in their workshop. They must be present and accounted for in these groups at the beginning of each workday. During the day, the inmates check out of their groups for various activities.*

*They check back in again when those activities have been completed. Assume that the day is divided into three activity periods.*

ROSTER OF INMATES

| GROUP X | Ted | Frank | George | Harry |
|---|---|---|---|---|
| GROUP Y | Jack | Ken | Larry | Mel |
| GROUP Z | Phil | Bob | Sam | Vic |

*The following table shows the movements of these inmates from their groups during the day. Assume that all were present and accounted for at the beginning of Period I.*

| | | GROUP X | GROUP Y | GROUP Z |
|---|---|---|---|---|
| Period I | Check-outs | Ted, Frank | Ken, Larry | Phil |
| Period II | Check-ins | Frank | Ken, Larry | Phil |
| | Check-outs | George | Jack, Mel | Bob, Sam, Vic |
| Period III | Check-ins | George | Mel, Jack | Sam, Bob, Vic |
| | Check-outs | Frank, Harry | Ken | Vic |

SAMPLE QUESTION: At the end of Period II, the inmates remaining in Group X were
- A. Ted, Frank, Harry
- B. Frank, Harry
- C. Ted, George
- D. Frank, Harry, George

During Period I, Ted and Frank were checked out from Group X. During Period II, Frank was checked back in, and George was checked out. Therefore, the members of the group remaining out are Ted and George. The two other members of the group, Frank and Harry, should be present. The correct answer is B.

17. At the end of Period I, the TOTAL number of inmates remaining in their own permanent groups was

    A. 8   B. 7   C. 6   D. 5

18. At the end of Period I, the inmates remaining in Group Z were

    A. George and Harry   B. Jack and Mel
    C. Bob, Sam, and Vic   D. Phil

19. At the end of Period II, the inmates remaining in Group Y were

    A. Ken and Larry   B. Jack, Ken, and Mel
    C. Jack and Ken   D. Ken, Mel, and Larry

20. At the end of Period II, the TOTAL number of inmates remaining in their own permanent groups was

    A. 8   B. 7   C. 6   D. 5

21. At the end of Period II, the inmates who were NOT present in Group Z were

    A. Phil, Bob, and Sam   B. Sam, Bob, and Vic
    C. Sam, Vic, and Phil   D. Vic, Phil, and Bob

22. At the end of Period III, the inmates remaining in Group Y were

　　A. Ted, Frank, and George　　　B. Jack, Mel, and Ken
　　C. Jack, Larry, and Mel　　　　D. Frank and Harry

23. At the end of Period III, the TOTAL number of inmates NOT present in their own permanent groups was

　　A. 4　　　B. 5　　　C. 6　　　D. 7

24. Of the 100 inmates in a certain cellblock, one-half were assigned to clean-up work, and one-fifth were assigned to work in the laundry.
How many inmates were NOT assigned for clean-up work or laundry work?

　　A. 30　　　B. 40　　　C. 50　　　D. 60

25. A certain cellblock has a maximum capacity of 250 inmates. On March 26, there were 200 inmates housed in the cellblock. 12 inmates were added on that day, and 17 inmates were added on the following day. No inmates left on either day.
How many more inmates could this cellblock have accommodated on the second day?

　　A. 11　　　B. 16　　　C. 21　　　D. 28

---

# KEY (CORRECT ANSWERS)

| | | | |
|---|---|---|---|
| 1. C | | 11. C | |
| 2. D | | 12. C | |
| 3. A | | 13. C | |
| 4. B | | 14. D | |
| 5. D | | 15. D | |
| 6. A | | 16. A | |
| 7. B | | 17. B | |
| 8. D | | 18. C | |
| 9. A | | 19. A | |
| 10. C | | 20. D | |

21. B
22. C
23. B
24. A
25. C

# TEST 2

DIRECTIONS: Each question or incomplete statement is followed by several suggested answers or completions. Select the one that BEST answers the question or completes the statement. *PRINT THE LETTER OF THE CORRECT ANSWER IN THE SPACE AT THE RIGHT.*

Questions 1-5.

DIRECTIONS: Questions 1 through 5 are to be answered SOLELY on the basis of the Report of Offense that appears below.

| REPORT OF OFFENSE | | Report No. | 26743 |
|---|---|---|---|
| | | Date of Report | 10-12 |
| Inmate | Joseph Brown | | |
| Age | 27 | Number | 61274 |
| Sentence | 90 days | Assignment | KU-187 |
| Place of Offense | R.P.W. 4-1 | Date of Offense | 10/11 |
| Offense | Assaulting inmate | | |
| Details | During 9:00 p.m. cellblock clean-up, inmate John Jones asked for pail being used by Brown. Brown refused. Correction officer requested that Brown comply. Brown then threw pail at Jones with intent to injure him and said he would "get" Jones. Jones not hurt. | | |
| Force Used by Officer | None | | |
| Name of Reporting Officer | R. Rodriguez | No. | C-2056 |
| Name of Superior Officer | P. Ferguson | | |

1. The person who made out this report is

   A. Joseph Brown  B. John Jones
   C. R. Rodriguez  D. P. Ferguson

2. Disregarding the details, the specific offense reported was

   A. insulting a fellow inmate
   B. assaulting a fellow inmate
   C. injuring a fellow inmate
   D. disobeying a correction officer

3. The number of the inmate who committed the offense is

   A. 26743   B. 61274   C. KU-187   D. C-2056

4. The offense took place on

   A. October 11   B. June 12
   C. December    D. November 13

5. The place where the offense occurred is identified in the report as

   A. Brown's cell   B. Jones' cell
   C. KU-187         D. R.P.W., 4-1

6. Add $51.79, $29.39, and $8.98.
   The CORRECT answer is

   A. $78.97   B. $88.96   C. $89.06   D. $90.16

7. Add $72.07 and $31.54, then subtract $25.75.
   The CORRECT answer is

   A. $77.86   B. $82.14   C. $88.96   D. $129.36

8. Start with $82.47, then subtract $25.50, $4.75, and 35¢.
   The CORRECT answer is

   A. $30.60   B. $51.87   C. $52.22   D. $65.25

9. Add $19.35 and $37.75, then subtract $9.90 and $19.80.
   The CORRECT answer is

   A. $27.40   B. $37.00   C. $37.30   D. $47.20

10. Multiply $38.85 by 2; then subtract $27.90.
    The CORRECT answer is

    A. $21.90   B. $48.70   C. $49.80   D. $50.70

11. Add $53.66, $9.27, and $18.75, then divide by 2.
    The CORRECT answer is

    A. $35.84   B. $40.34   C. $40.84   D. $41.34

12. Out of 192 inmates in a certain cellblock, 96 are to go on a work detail and another 32 are to report to a vocational class. All the rest are to remain in the cellblock.
    How many inmates should be left on the cellblock?

    A. 48   B. 64   C. 86   D. 128

13. Assume that you, as a correction officer, are responsible for seeing that the right number of utensils are counted out for a meal. You need enough utensils for 620 men. One fork and one spoon are needed for each man. In addition, one ladle is needed for each group of 20 men.
    How many utensils will be needed altogether?

    A. 1240   B. 1271   C. 1550   D. 1860

14. Assume that you, as a correction officer, are supervising the inmates who are assigned to a dishwashing detail. There is a direct relationship between the amount of time it takes to do all the dishwashing and the number of inmates who are washing dishes. When two inmates are washing dishes, the job takes six hours.
    If there are four inmates washing dishes, how long should the job take?
    _____ hour(s).

    A. 1   B. 2   C. 3   D. 4

15. Assume that you, as a correction officer, are in charge of supervising the laundry sorting and counting. You expect that on a certain day there will be nearly 7,000 items to be sorted and counted.
    If one inmate can sort and count 500 items in an hour, how many inmates are needed to sort all 7,000 items in one hour?

    A. 2  B. 5  C. 7  D. 14

16. A carpentry course is being given for inmates who want to learn a skill. The course will be taught in several different groups. Each group should contain at least 12 but not more than 16 men. The smaller the group, the better, as long as there are at least 12 men per group. If 66 inmates are going to take the course, they should be divided into

    A. 4 groups of 16 men
    B. 4 groups of 13 men and 1 group of 14 men
    C. 3 groups of 13 men and 2 groups of 14 men
    D. 6 groups of 11 men

Questions 17-21.

DIRECTIONS: Questions 17 through 21 are to be answered on the basis of the Fact Situation and the Report of Inmate Injury form below. The questions ask how the report form should be filled in, based on the information given in the Fact Situation.

### FACT SITUATION

*Peter Miller is a correction officer assigned to duty in Cellblock A. His superior officer is John Doakes. Miller was on duty at 1:30 P.M. on March 21, 2004, when he heard a scream for help from Cell 12. He hurried to Cell 12 and found inmate Richard Rogers stamping out a flaming book of matches. Inmate John Jones was screaming. It seems that Jones had accidentally set fire to the entire book of matches while lighting a cigarette, and he had burned his left hand. Smoking was permitted at this hour. Miller reported the incident by phone, and Jones was escorted to the dispensary where his hand was treated at 2:00 P.M. by Dr. Albert Lorillo. Dr. Lorillo determined that Jones could return to his cellblock, but that he should be released from work for four days. The doctor scheduled a re-examination for March 22. A routine investigation of the incident was made by James Lopez. Jones confirmed to this officer that the above statement of the situation was correct.*

```
                    REPORT OF INMATE INJURY
(1)  Name of Inmate _____    (2)  Assignment _____
(3)  Number _____    (4)  Location _____
(5)  Nature of Injury _____   (6)  Date _____
(7)  Details (how, when, where injury was incurred) _____
(8)  Received medical attention:     Date _____   Time _____
(9)  Treatment _____
(10) Disposition ( check one or more):
        ___ (10-1) Return to housing area      ___ (10-2) Return to duty
        ___ (10-3) Work release ___ days       ___ (10-4) Re-examine in
                                                          ___ days
(11) Employing reporting injury _____
(12) Employee's supervisor or superior officer _____
(13) Medical officer treating injury _____
(14) Investigating officer _____
(15) Head of institution _____
```

17. Which of the following should be entered in Item 1?

    A. Peter Miller           B. John Doakes
    C. Richard Rogers         D. John Jones

18. Which of the following should be entered in Item 11?

    A. Peter Miller           B. James Lopez
    C. Richard Rogers         D. John Jones

19. Which of the following should be entered in Item 8?

    A. 2/21/04, 1:30 P.M.     B. 2/21/04, 2:00 P.M.
    C. 3/21/04, 1:30 P.M.     D. 3/21/04, 2:00 P.M.

20. For Item 10, which of the following should be checked?

    A. Only 10-4              B. 10-1 and 10-4
    C. 10-1, 10-3, and 10-4   D. 10-2, 10-3, and 10-4

21. Of the following items, which one CANNOT be filled in on the basis of the information given in the Fact Situation?
    Item _____.

    A. 12        B. 13        C. 14        D. 15

Questions 22-25.

DIRECTIONS: Questions 22 through 25 are to be answered on the basis of the chart which appears on the following page. The chart shows an 8-hour schedule for 4 groups of inmates. The numbers across the top of the chart stand for hours of the day: the hour beginning at 8:00, the hour beginning at 9:00, and so forth. The exact number of men in each group is given at the lefthand side of the chart. An hour when the men in a particular group are scheduled to be OUT of their cellblock is marked with an X.

|  | 8 | 9 | 10 | 11 | 12 | 1 | 2 | 3 |
|---|---|---|---|---|---|---|---|---|
| GROUP Q 44 men | X |  | X |  |  | X |  |  |
| GROUP R 60 men | X |  | X | X |  | X | X |  |
| GROUP S 24 men | X |  |  |  | X |  |  |  |
| GROUP T 28 men | X |  | X |  | X |  |  |  |

22. How many of the men were in their cellblock from 11:00 to 12:00?  22.____
    A. 60   B. 96   C. 104   D. 156

23. At 10:45, how many of the men were NOT in their cellblock?  23.____
    A. 24   B. 60   C. 96   D. 132

24. At 12:30, what proportion of the men were NOT in their cellblock?  24.____
    A. 1/4   B. 1/3   C. 1/2   D. 2/3

25. During the period covered in the chart, what percentage of the time did the men in Group S spend in their cellblock?  25.____
    A. 60%   B. 65%   C. 70%   D. 75%

# KEY (CORRECT ANSWERS)

1. C    11. C
2. B    12. B
3. B    13. B
4. A    14. C
5. D    15. D

6. D    16. B
7. A    17. D
8. B    18. A
9. A    19. D
10. C   20. C

21. D
22. B
23. D
24. B
25. D

# EXAMINATION SECTION
# TEST 1

DIRECTIONS: Each question or incomplete statement is followed by several suggested answers or completions. Select the one that BEST answers the question or completes the statement. *PRINT THE LETTER OF THE CORRECT ANSWER IN THE SPACE AT THE RIGHT.*

1. The shift from an individual to a formal response of crime resulted in which one of the following:  1.____

    A. Elimination of revenge
    B. Made punishment more humane
    C. Lessened the chances of longstanding family feuds
    D. Promoted citizen disinterest in crime and the punishment of criminals
    E. Contributed to the development of a more just method of determining guilt

2. The MOST important trend in corrections today:  2.____

    A. Attempt to reinforce any ties between the offender and the community
    B. Long sentences
    C. Less use of confinement if possible
    D. Developing programs for prisoners in prisons
    E. None of the above

3. People commit crimes because  3.____

    A. they are mentally ill
    B. they come from poor families
    C. it is their way of trying to solve their problems
    D. they want to
    E. they are born criminals

4. The jail officer's role in the jail is to  4.____
    I. represent the sheriff
    II. represent the criminal justice system
    III. assume responsibility for the welfare of prisoners
    IV. punish prisoners for their crimes
    V. appease social pressure
   The CORRECT answer is:

    A. I, II
    B. II, III
    C. I, II, III
    D. II, III, IV
    E. II, V

5. Which one of the following is a *genuine* characteristic of a professional jail officer? He  5.____

    A. becomes easily upset by prisoners
    B. wants to punish prisoners for their crimes
    C. tries to treat all prisoners alike without favoritism or emotion
    D. refuses to discuss the prisoners' guilt or innocence
    E. is critical of the courts and the law and says so to prisoners

2 (#1)

# KEY (CORRECT ANSWERS)

1. E
2. A
3. C
4. B
5. C

# TEST 2

DIRECTIONS: Each question or incomplete statement is followed by several suggested answers or completions. Select the one that BEST answers the question or completes the statement. *PRINT THE LETTER OF THE CORRECT ANSWER IN THE SPACE AT THE RIGHT.*

1. From the list below, select the one that is legally proper on which the jail officer can book a prisoner:

   A. Larceny
   B. Hold for Dr. Jones
   C. False identification
   D. Suspicion
   E. Hold for investigation

2. The purpose of a strip search is:
   I. To discover contraband
   II. To let the prisoner know that he is now in jail
   III. To discover if he has lice
   IV. To appraise physical condition
   V. All of the above

   The CORRECT answer is:

   A. I, II
   B. II, III
   C. I, IV
   D. I, III
   E. V

3. Select those statements that are TRUE about strip and frisk searches:
   I. If you are not certain that you examined an area, return to it
   II. All searches should be systematic
   III. An incomplete search is as bad as no search at all
   IV. Your attitude when conducting the search is as important as the way the search is done
   V. All of the above

   The CORRECT answer is:

   A. I, III
   B. II, III
   C. II, III, IV
   D. I, III, IV
   E. V

4. Identification procedures are important because:
   I. The FBI requires them
   II. It is a method of identifying those persons who are wanted by other jurisdictions
   III. It is a method of identifying prisoners when they are released
   IV. It is necessary for statistical purposes
   V. All of the above

   The CORRECT answer is:

   A. II, III
   B. I, IV
   C. II, IV
   D. I, II
   E. V

5. Physical examinations for all prisoners at the time of admission are

   A. a waste of time since most of them are drunks anyway
   B. necessary to discover the sick and injured
   C. necessary only if a prisoner seems to be obviously sick
   D. duplicatory of previous physicals

6. Which of the following are NOT accurate descriptions of personal property and should not be used?
   I. Gold watch
   II. Plaid sport coat, size 40
   III. Yellow metal ring with diamond
   IV. Brown suit, Bonds label, hole in left elbow, trousers soiled at right knee, size 40
   V. Timex watch

   The CORRECT answer is:

   A. I, II, V
   B. II, III, V
   C. I, IV, V
   D. I, II, III
   E. I, III, V

7. Bathing of all prisoners when they are admitted to the jail is necessary for the following reasons:
   I. It is good for staff morale to see clean prisoners
   II. Prevent vermin from entering the jail
   III. No one likes dirty people
   IV. It contributes to the health and well-being of prisoners
   V. All of the above

   The CORRECT answer is:

   A. I, II
   B. II, III
   C. III, IV
   D. II, IV
   E. V

8. Prisoners should not be permitted to wear long hair because

   A. it is unsightly
   B. it is unsanitary
   C. the jail staff do not like it
   D. all of the above
   E. none of the above

9. All prisoners should wear jail clothing because

   A. they look neater when they all are dressed alike
   B. it is a good security procedure since it makes escape difficult
   C. it is simpler for them to do their laundry
   D. it is cheaper

10. Match the following descriptions of prisoners with the appropriate housing assignment:

    A. Juvenile prisoner
    B. Elderly or infirm prisoner
    C. Mentally ill prisoner
    D. Hostile aggressive prisoner

    1. dormitory, near infirmary
    2. in single cell away from all adults
    3. in a single cell
    4. in a single cell under close supervision
    5. in a padded cell

11. The PROPER definition of contraband is:  11.____

    A. Any item that can be used as a weapon, and all drugs
    B. All items listed as contraband and posted in the jail
    C. All items not issued by the jail and not specifically authorized
    D. Illicit guns.

12. Cell searches are necessary for the following reason:  12.____

    A. To discover contraband        B. To keep prisoners off balance
    C. To reduce clutter             D. All of the above

13. Identify the two MOST important principles of a cell search:  13.____
    I.   Examine everything in the cell
    II.  Be systematic
    III. Leave the cell in the same condition in which it was found
    IV.  Ignore the prisoner when searching his cell
    V.   Remain aloof
    The CORRECT answer is:

    A. I, II          B. II, III          C. III, IV
    D. IV, V          E. I, III

14. Indicate whether the following statements are TRUE or FALSE:  14.

    A. Counts are unnecessary if prisoners are locked up at all times.        A.____
    B. A jail officer should know how many prisoners he has at all times.     B.____
    C. One officer can make an accurate count in a dormitory.                 C.____
    D. Roll call counts are easy to take and make good sense.                 D.____
    E. When counting prisoners, the officer must always see flesh.            E.____
    F. It is not good practice to permit prisoners to conduct a count         F.____

15. Select the statements that are examples of good key control:  15.____
    I.   Since minimum security prisoners can be trusted, it is proper to permit them
         to use keys to unlock and lock all doors
    II.  A jail officer should never carry both inside and outside keys
    III. Jail officers should be permitted to exchange keys during shift change
    IV.  All security keys should be concealed when carried
    V.   None of the above
    The CORRECT answer is:

    A. I, III         B. II, III          C. II, IV
    D. I, IV          E. V

16. The single MOST effective security measure in the jail is  16.____

    A. remote TV camera              B. tool-hardened steel
    C. metal detectors               D. the alertness of the jail officer
    E. stoolies

17. Indicate whether the following statements are TRUE or FALSE:

    A. Weapons are needed in the jail in order to protect personnel
    B. Gas in aerosol cans and clubs are not weapons
    C. The weapon carried in the jail by the officer can be taken away and used against him
    D. Although all jail personnel should be required to check their weapons before entering the jail, FBI agents and visiting sheriffs are exempt
    E. The armory should be inside the jail so that weapons will be available to jail officers when they need them

## KEY (CORRECT ANSWERS)

1. A
2. D
3. C
4. A
5. B
6. E
7. D
8. E
9. B
10. A. 2
    B. 1
    C. 4
    D. 3
11. C
12. A
13. B
14. A. F
    B. T
    C. F
    D. F
    E. T
    F. T
15. C
16. D
17. A. F
    B. F
    C. T
    D. F
    E. F

# TEST 3

DIRECTIONS: Each question or incomplete statement is followed by several suggested answers or completions. Select the one that BEST answers the question or completes the statement. *PRINT THE LETTER OF THE CORRECT ANSWER IN THE SPACE AT THE RIGHT.*

1. What are the two MOST important changes that occur when a prisoner is admitted to the jail? He   1._____

    A. becomes a prisoner
    B. changes status from citizen to prisoner
    C. has to wear jail clothing
    D. begins to lose his identity

2. List the *tangible* items that contribute to a prisoner's identity and that are taken from him when he enters the jail. (List six.)   2._____

    1. _____   2. _____
    3. _____   4. _____
    5. _____   6. _____

3. List the *intangibles* that contribute to a prisoner's identity that he loses when he enters the jail. (List three.)   3._____

    1. _____   2. _____   3. _____

4. Indicate whether the following statements are TRUE or FALSE:   4.

    A. Prisoners are generally not frustrated by their inability to do things for themselves because they have few things bothering them.   A._____
    B. Giving a prisoner good conduct time is equal to rewards he would receive in the community such as pay, approval, and responsibility.   B._____
    C. Cutting a prisoner's hair at admission does not alter his identity.   C._____
    D. A prisoner's sudden dependence on his wife and friends does not change his relationship with them.   D._____
    E. There is no similarity between the feelings a prisoner has when confined and the person who is entering military service.   E._____

5. The newly admitted prisoner can be assisted in adjusting to the jail by one of the following methods:   5._____

    A. Orientation by other prisoners
    B. Written rules and regulations that are given to him
    C. Trial and error and by watching others
    D. Kept in a cell until he learns jail routine

6. Although any period in confinement can be considered a critical time, the following times are especially sensitive: (Select two.)   6._____

    A. During discharge of the prisoner from the jail
    B. During searches of cells
    C. During strip or frisk searches
    D. Immediately before or after court appearances
    E. During mealtimes
    F. All of the above

19

7. What should be done about a prisoner who appears hostile during admission?

   A. Lock him up in a cell immediately
   B. Insist on carrying out the admission procedure and ask the arresting officer to assist you
   C. Be certain to get all the details of the arrest and the prisoner's behavior from the arresting officer. This should be done in the presence of the prisoner so that he knows he can't fool you.
   D. Get rid of the arresting officer as soon as possible. Carry out the admission procedure calmly and quietly.

8. The BEST procedure to follow when a prisoner is upset from a visit from his wife or girlfriend is to do the following:

   A. Lock him in a cell by himself so that he will not try to escape and where he will not disturb others
   B. Permit him to call his wife or girlfriend and correct the misunderstanding
   C. Talk to the prisoner or at least be a sympathetic and understanding listener
   D. If he is continuously having problems because of argument with visitors, refuse to let further visits to take place

9. Although many factors are involved in setting and controlling the jail climate, the MOST important is:

   A. The behavior of the prisoners since they can be hostile and manipulative
   B. The attitude and behavior of the staff
   C. The quality of the food
   D. Relaxed security procedures
   E. All of the above

10. The following technique is useful in avoiding prisoner manipulation:

    A. Refuse to discuss any prisoner's problems with him
    B. Establish good communications with other staff members
    C. Keep good records
    D. Ignore prisoner complaints and refuse to permit any exceptions to jail rules

11. Indicate whether the following statements are TRUE or FALSE:

    A. A suicide attempt is usually an attempt to manipulate jail staff
    B. Overreacting to prisoners is an indication that the jail officer is conscientious and concerned
    C. A jail officer should always act knowledgeable about jail procedures even when he is not
    D. Jail rules seldom need to be changed; they do need to be updated by adding new rules from time to time
    E. There is nothing wrong with rules made up by prisoners because usually they are tougher than rules developed by the administrator

12. A jail officer who overreacts to prisoners is 12.____
    A. alert to prisoner manipulation
    B. demonstrating an interest in his work
    C. lacks confidence and is insecure
    D. all of the above

13. List characteristics of the trained, professional jailer: (List seven.) 13.____
    1. _____    2. _____
    3. _____    4. _____
    5. _____    6. _____
    7. _____

14. Indicate whether the following statements are TRUE or FALSE: 14.
    A. A jail officer who disagrees with a jail rule and lets prisoners know it will be considered an honest officer and will be contributing to a positive jail climate    A.____
    B. The jail officer who gossips with prisoners gets their respect because he is demonstrating that he is just like they are    B.____
    C. Discussing dissatisfactions about the jail with prisoners is a good way to get good suggestions for changes in jail policy    C.____
    D. Prisoners are quick to interpret differences of opinion between staff members as signs of disunity    D.____
    E. Regulations assist prisoners in adjusting to the jail by eliminating confusion    E.____
    F. Rigid rules are the most effective way of keeping order and contribute to a well-run jail and few disciplinary reports    F.____
    G. Vague regulations are an indication to prisoners that personnel do not have clear understanding or control of the jail    G.____
    H. Reasonable rules reduce staff-prisoner conflict    H.____

# KEY (CORRECT ANSWERS)

1. B, D
2. Street clothing, haircut, jewelry, belt, tie clip, cigarette lighter
3. Work, relations with his family, daily habits
4. A. F
   B. F
   C. F
   D. F
   E. F
5. B
6. C, D
7. D
8. C
9. B
10. B
11. A. F
    B. F
    C. F
    D. F
    E. F
12. C
13. Flexibility, self-confidence, willingness to make decisions, impartiality, refusal to respond in a hostile manner to prisoner hostility, respect for himself and his work, willingness to perform all necessary tasks
14. A. F
    B. F
    C. F
    D. T
    E. T
    F. F
    G. T
    H. T

# TEST 4

DIRECTIONS: Each question or incomplete statement is followed by several suggested answers or completions. Select the one that BEST answers the question or completes the statement. *PRINT THE LETTER OF THE CORRECT ANSWER IN THE SPACE AT THE RIGHT.*

1. Select the one statement that completes the following sentence.  
   The overall objective of supervision is

   A. achievement of security
   B. protection of prisoners
   C. teaching prisoners how to work
   D. the development of an orderly environment

   1._____

2. Another important goal of supervision is control. This means:

   A. Making certain that each prisoner is either locked in his cell or under the direct physical control of the jail officer
   B. That jail officers closely supervise prisoner activities, especially where trusties are in charge of other prisoners
   C. That jail personnel supervise all prisoners, develop procedures, set standards, and evaluate results
   D. All of the above

   2._____

3. An officer is placed on a new assignment where he will be supervising prisoners. Which of the following is the proper FIRST step he should take in assuming this assignment?

   A. Call the prisoners together and tell them what kind of work he expects from them.
   B. Ask the prisoners for suggestions on how this particular operation can be improved.
   C. Ask each prisoner for a description of his work so that he can seek ways to revise procedures and make them more effective.
   D. Read post orders, familiarize himself with policies and procedures, and learn all he can about the assignment.

   3._____

4. Officer P assigned four prisoners to a small empty cell block and gave them the following instructions. *I want this place cleaned up. I'll be back before the end of the day to check on your work.*  
   List the errors made by Officer P. (List three.)

   1. _____
   2. _____
   3. _____

   4._____

5. A supervisor is responsible for making an accurate and honest evaluation of a prisoner's performance.  
   In order to do this, he must

   A. know a great deal about the prisoner, including his offense, his family life, and his education
   B. have supervised him long enough to know him well

   5._____

23

C. recognize and account for individual differences
D. evaluate all prisoners as working equally hard or satisfactorily
E. recognize either improvement or a change for the worse and, if possible, explain it

6. Select the two statements that demonstrate a supervisor's objectivity in evaluating a prisoner:

   A. This man is lazy
   B. This man is always at the end of the line when picking up tools and first in line when turning them in
   C. Prisoner J is one of the slowest moving men in the crew
   D. Prisoner A is hard working, energetic, and always on the go
   E. Prisoner S listens carefully, asks questions when he does not understand, and makes few mistakes

7. Officer R is trying hard to do a good job. He feels that it is important for jail officers to communicate with prisoners. In this way, he can keep in touch with them and their problems and, as a result, will be a more effective supervisor. This morning he came in and in talking to some of the prisoners commented that he certainly was tired; he should not have stayed out so late. Not only was he tired, but his wife was angry with him because of the late hours he keeps when bowling.
   One of the prisoners asked him about his score. He replied that he averaged 105. One of the prisoners commented that this was a lady's score, and the other prisoners laughed.
   What errors did Officer R make? (List three.)

   1. _____
   2. _____
   3. _____

8. Officer S has been talking to Prisoner O. During the conversation, O says, *"Don't you think that Idiot T would know better than to loan I cigarettes when he knows I is leaving before commissary day?"* Officer S replied, *"I never did think T had too many brains and now I'm certain of it. But then, I doesn't have too many smarts either."* What do you think Prisoner O is thinking of Officer S's remarks? (Select one.)

   A. Well, we seem to agree about some things.
   B. Gee, Officer S is pretty sharp about who is smart or dumb.
   C. I wonder what he says about me to other prisoners.
   D. He is right about T but I think I is a smart old bird. But I'm not going to argue with him.

9. Prisoner B is having problems with his wife. She wants to have their eight-year-old boy's tonsils removed, and B wants her to wait until he is released. He is discussing the problem with Officer R who tells him, *"Listen, "let her have them removed. The sooner the better; it's like pulling a tooth, fast and simple."*
   Do you think this advice was good or bad? (Select one.)

   A. *Good;* it will keep the wife occupied while Prisoner B is in jail.
   B. *Good;* the boy should have his tonsils removed.
   C. *Bad;* Officer R knows nothing about the family situation or the boy's medical condition.

D. *Bad;* he is taking the wife's side in the argument.
E. *Good;* he is giving the prisoner advice, and the prisoner needs it if he is to resolve his problem.

10. The Lockmeup County Jail is run simply and with little fuss or bother. The sheriff has found that the prisoners can pretty well take care of themselves. The jail is fairly clean and seems to be quite orderly. It seems, however, that some prisoners never do any work and always have money, cigarettes, and commissary.
What is going on here?

    A. The prisoners are probably a well-behaved, cooperative group who are interested in getting along with the sheriff.
    B. It is highly probable that prisoners are running the jail and have established a sanitary court.
    C. Both of the above
    D. None of the above

10.____

11. Officer J has assigned three prisoners to the kitchen detail to wash pots, mop the floor, and wipe tables. He will not be available to supervise them at all times. He has, therefore, given one of the prisoners responsibility for organizing the work and giving out assignments.
Is Officer J making any supervisory errors?

    A. *No;* a good supervisor learns to delegate responsibility.
    B. *Yes;* prisoners should never have any supervisory responsibility over other prisoners.
    C. *No;* he will be checking them from time to time so there is little chance that anything will go wrong.
    D. *Yes;* he has not been clear in his assignment of work.

11.____

12. Officer P is responsible for the supervision of a cell block during the evening hours when there is little activity in the jail. His post is at the door to the cell block, but he makes it a habit to make rounds of the cell block once every hour. His tour always takes place during the last 15 minutes of the hour. Officer P believes in being systematic and organized. This evening Prisoner S asked him for a light and engaged him in conversation. S is usually not talkative. The other prisoners lounging in the bullpen area between cells seemed somewhat noisier than usual, but not to the point where it would be disturbing.
What do you think could be happening in the cell block?

    A. Nothing; it is not unusual for prisoners to change and become friendly. In fact, S's desire to talk should be encouraged; perhaps in time he may want to discuss his problems with Officer P.
    B. An escape is in progress, and the prisoners are trying to provide a distraction.
    C. These distractions could cover an escape attempt or sexual assaults in another part of the jail.
    D. Nothing; the prisoner usually becomes a little noisy as the evening progresses.

12.____

13. Referring to Question 12 above, do you think Officer P is making any errors?

    A. *No;* he is responding to a prisoner's need to talk to someone.
    B. *Yes;* he should not make his tours through the cell block according to such a rigid schedule.

13.____

C. *No*; he seems to be alert and is actively supervising the cell block.
D. *Yes*; he should not be giving S a light.

14. The television set for prisoners is located in the day-room. Although it had been possible to buy the set with remote controls, this was not done.
How do you think the jail staff can ensure that they will exercise control over the set?
   I. The threat of losing the television will be enough to keep the prisoners in line.
   II. The on-off switch should be controlled by the jail staff.
   III. The prisoners should be permitted to set up a committee to develop rules for television use.
   IV. Jail staff should set viewing hours and have the final approval over programs.
   The CORRECT answer is:

   A. I, II          B. II, III          C. I, IV
   D. III, IV        E. II, IV

15. The jail is switching over to dining room feeding. This has been made possible by the addition of eight jail officers.
Where should the posts be located to cover the trouble spots?

   A. Along the walls of the dining room
   B. Circulating in the dining room
   C. One watching the line entering the dining room, one in the kitchen, and the other circulating
   D. One at the line entering the dining room, one at the serving line, one at the silverware collection and tray scraping can, and three either along the wall or circulating

16. List the important points in supervising the feeding of prisoners in their cells. (List four.)

   1. _____
   2. _____
   3. _____
   4. _____

17. Although the jail has a routine procedure for handling sick call, Officer P has worked out a much simpler system. Whenever a prisoner requests to see the doctor, Officer P questions him; and if the prisoner complains of a headache or cold, he is given two aspirin. This has reduced the sick call line substantially. Officer P prides himself in his ability to handle sick call requests and to spot the chronic complainers.
Do you feel that Officer P's behavior is proper?
   I. No; jail officers should not give out medication.
   II. Yes; doctors are busy and reducing the number of sick call requests will help them give more time to those who are really sick.
   III. No; Officer P is diagnosing prisoner medical complaints, and he is not qualified to do this.
   IV. Yes, as long as he limits his medical activity to those who have colds and headaches.
   V. Yes; after all, the prisoners are diagnosing their condition by telling Officer P that they have colds or headaches. Furthermore, aspirin is not medicine.

   The CORRECT answer is:

   A. I, III         B. I, II          C. III, IV
   D. I, IV          E. III, V

18. List the five BASIC principles of supervising prisoners on sick call and during their medical care.

    1. _____
    2. _____
    3. _____
    4. _____
    5. _____

19. Supervising visiting is a dull assignment to Officer K. He manages to pass the time by concentrating on the visiting couple who are seated nearest him. Usually, he overhears some interesting conversations. Visiting in this jail is done in a room with tables that have a four-inch partition running through their center. Today, Officer K became so interested in the visit of the prisoner and his girlfriend seated near him that he didn't realize that he was permitting them and other prisoners to visit longer than regulations allowed.
    Do you think Officer K has made any errors?
    I. No; he was giving close supervision to the visitors.
    II. Yes; it is not his responsibility to eavesdrop on visitors' conversations.
    III. No; permitting visiting to last longer than regulations allow is not an error.
    IV. Yes; he was distracted by one visitor and did not pay any attention to other visiting taking place.
    The CORRECT answer is:

    A. III, IV  B. III, V  C. II, IV
    D. I, II    E. II, III

20. Which of the following descriptive statements are included in a definition of a trusty. A trusty

    A. is a prisoner who can be trusted to work without supervision
    B. is a prisoner who can work under minimum supervision
    C. can be depended on not to escape
    D. is a prisoner who because he can be trusted can be given responsibility to supervise the work of other prisoners and lock and unlock cells. He thus makes the work of jail personnel much easier.

21. What *special* privileges should trusties have that are NOT permitted to other prisoners?

    A. Freedom to move about in the jail without special permission
    B. Extra food because they work
    C. Permitted to run errands for jail personnel
    D. They should not have any special privileges

22. A prisoner being considered for trusty status should be evaluated in three areas. Indicate by writing in the kinds of information that should be examined. (List three kinds.)

    1. _____
    2. _____
    3. _____

23. Why must juveniles be kept separate from adult prisoners? (List two reasons.) 23.____

    1. _____
    2. _____

24. In what way is supervision of women DIFFERENT from supervision for men? 24.____

    _____
    _____
    _____
    _____

25. Officer W has been supervising the recreation periods recently. Yesterday, he overruled 25.____
    the umpire's decision even though there had been no argument from either team. There
    was little doubt that the umpire had made a bad call. Today, he took part in a volleyball
    game in order to even sides.
    Do you feel Officer W has made any errors?

    A. *No;* he is correcting the umpire and thus avoiding complaints or arguments from
       prisoners.
    B. *Yes;* it seems that the prisoner did not contest the call.
    C. *Yes;* he is becoming involved with prisoner recreation activities when there is no
       need to do so, and he is ignoring his supervisory responsibility.
    D. *No;* a supervisor should be alert to possible problems and try and solve them
       before they become serious. Correcting the umpire was correct. He is also con-
       tributing to the recreation period by participating in the game.

26. List the BASIC principles of supervising a prisoner at a funeral or other social activity out- 26.____
    side the jail. (List three.)

    1. _____
    2. _____
    3. _____

# KEY (CORRECT ANSWERS)

1. D
2. C
3. D
4. Poor directions - too general; did not take into account the possibility that some of the prisoners may not have understood his orders; is not making periodic cheeks.
5. C
6. B, E
7. A. Discussed his off-duty activities with prisoners.
   B. Discussed his relationship with his wife with prisoners.
   C. Mention of the bowling score was not important, but this was an opening for the prisoners to make an insulting remark.
8. C
9. C
10. B
11. B
12. C
13. B
14. E
15. D
16. A. Deliver food while it is hot
    B. Supervisor must accompany the prisoner who is serving food
    C. Count utensils to and from prisoners
    D. Make seconds available as a means of preventing stronger prisoners from stealing food from the weak.
17. A
18. A. Do not diagnose.
    B. Supervise prisoners closely when they are taking medication.
    C. Never give out more than one dose of medication at one time.
    D. Keep accurate medical records.
    E. Permit all prisoners' sick call requests.
19. C
20. B
21. D
22. A. Escape record and detainers
    B. Work habits
    C. Behavior in confinement
23. A. To prevent adults from possibly sexually assaulting them.
    B. To keep juveniles from being exposed to hardened criminal types
24. There is no basic difference. The same principles and techniques can be used. Women must be kept separate from male prisoners.
25. C
26. A. Do not remove cuffs unless prior approval has been given by the jail administrator.
    B. Keep the prisoner in sight at all times.
    C. No special visits or other requests to be granted.

# TEST 5

DIRECTIONS: Each question or incomplete statement is followed by several suggested answers or completions. Select the one that BEST answers the question or completes the statement. *PRINT THE LETTER OF THE CORRECT ANSWER IN THE SPACE AT THE RIGHT.*

1. The GOAL of discipline in jail is to

   A. teach prisoners absolute obedience to orders
   B. teach acceptable behavior
   C. teach prisoners self-control
   D. control prisoners

2. Written rules serve the following purposes:
   I. To inform prisoners what not to do
   II. To inform prisoners about what is expected of them
   III. To establish standards for evaluating prisoners' conduct
   IV. Take authority away from jail officers who should be responsible for establishing standards of conduct

   The CORRECT answer is:

   A. I, II   B. I, III   C. II, IV
   D. III, IV   E. II, III

3. Officer O has a temper that he displays whenever a prisoner gets on his nerves. He insists that prisoners do what they are told and that they follow the rules to the letter. It is his opinion that generally people get into trouble with the law because they lack discipline. He feels that it is his responsibility to teach prisoners discipline.
   Do you feel that Officer O is CORRECT?

   A. *Yes;* prisoners will generally take advantage of an officer who is not very strict.
   B. *No;* Officer O is too strict. He probably antagonizes prisoners by his attitude.
   C. *Yes;* all jail officers have a responsibility to teach prisoners discipline.
   D. *Yes;* however, he certainly sets a poor example by his display of temper.

4. Officer A caught two prisoners horsing around and decided to punish them by making them run in place. He reasoned that this would tire them so that they would not have the energy for horseplay.
   Do you think his actions were PROPER?

   A. *Yes;* prisoners learn a lesson from immediate punishment.
   B. *No;* the officer who sees the infraction should not, as a rule, also decide the punishment.
   C. Both of the above
   D. None of the above

5. Officer S is a firm believer in keeping order. He practices this belief and, as a result, turns in a high number of disciplinary reports.
   Do you think that S is acting properly?

   A. *Yes;* all infractions of rules should be reported.
   B. *No;* he should only report infractions that are serious and that cannot be handled informally.
   C. Both of the above
   D. None of the above

6. The following is a list of rule violations. Indicate those that require formal action and those that may be handled informally. (Use letter F for formal and letter I for informal.)

    A. Loud and continuous noise
    B. Talking after lights out
    C. Horseplay in sick call line
    D. Arguing with waiter in serving line
    E. Evidence of bar tampering
    F. Contraband (knife)
    G. Contraband (money)
    H. Contraband (book)
    I. Holding up line when returning to cells

6.
A. ____
B. ____
C. ____
D. ____
E. ____
F. ____
G. ____
H. ____
I. ____

7. Officer D has taken Prisoner E out of line for horseplay and is correcting him before a group of interested prisoners. What do you think are the possible consequences of this action?

    A. Prisoner E will learn a lesson.
    B. Prisoner E may become angry at being embarrassed in front of other prisoners.
    C. Officer D has realized that this was an excellent opportunity to teach E proper behavior and will make a positive impression on the prisoner.
    D. The other prisoners will also have an opportunity to learn from Prisoner E's experience.

7. ____

8. Prisoner O became abusive toward another prisoner, and they were on the edge of fighting when Officer C arrived on the scene. Both prisoners continued to argue, and a shoving contest began.
What should Officer C do?

    A. Step between the prisoners and separate them.
    B. Grab Prisoner O and pull him away.
    C. Shout to both prisoners to stop.
    D. He had better call another officer for assistance and then step in.

8. ____

9. Officer S is a large man and quite sure of himself. Today, when Prisoner N refused to come out of his cell to take a shower, Officer S went in and took him out.
Do you think this was the proper method?

    A. *Yes;* prisoners should do what they are told.
    B. *No;* the prisoner should have been permitted to remain in his cell until he decided to come out.
    C. *Yes;* prisoners must conform to all schedules.
    D. If it was necessary that Prisoner N come out of his cell, the officer should not have gone in alone to take him out.

9. ____

10. Prisoner N has declared that he is on a hunger strike and has refused to eat three meals in a row. A number of officers are upset by N's behavior and feel that something should be done about him.
Which do you feel is the PROPER procedure?

    A. Force feed him; all prisoners should eat three meals a day.
    B. Ignore him; he will eat when he is hungry.
    C. Wait a few days; and if he continues to refuse food, he should be force fed.
    D. Refer him to the doctor who can make a decision if and when he will require any medical care and forced feeding.

10.____

## KEY (CORRECT ANSWERS)

1. C
2. E
3. D
4. B
5. B

6. Formal: E, F, G, H
    Informal: A, B, C, D
7. B
8. D
9. D
10. D

# TEST 6

DIRECTIONS: Each question or incomplete statement is followed by several suggested answers or completions. Select the one that BEST answers the question or completes the statement. *PRINT THE LETTER OF THE CORRECT ANSWER IN THE SPACE AT THE RIGHT.*

1. A prisoner is brought to the jail with the following symptoms: shakiness, staggering, thick speech, and a blank glassy-eyed look.
Select the PROPER action to be taken.  1.____

   A. He is drunk; place him in the drunk tank.
   B. Although he may be drunk, it is possible that he may have a serious injury or illness. He should be referred to a doctor.
   C. Both of the above
   D. None of the above

2. Shortly after being admitted, a prisoner begins to shake, does not talk clearly, and claims to see bugs crawling over him.
The jailer should do one of the following:  2.____

   A. The prisoner is obviously psychotic and should be referred to the doctor
   B. The prisoner is having *DTs;* the doctor should be called immediately
   C. Although the prisoner is acting strangely, he should be observed for a time until it is obvious that he is sick
   D. None of the above

3. Prisoner E has been in jail two weeks waiting trial. Lately, he has been acting strangely. He has been talking to an imaginary person, laughing and arguing. Today he accused Officer T of trying to *get him.*
What should the officer do?  3.____

   A. Observe Prisoner E and submit a report to the administrator for medical referral
   B. Warn E to quiet down because he is disturbing others
   C. Try to prove to Prisoner E that the officer is not trying to get him
   D. None of the above

4. Prisoner L seems to have a habit of talking to himself, especially when he is playing solitaire. During the last week, he has also been complaining about his physical condition, claiming that he has a bad heart and that he is afraid it will stop one of these days soon.
What should the officer do?  4.____

   A. It seems that L is becoming psychotic; he should be referred to the doctor.
   B. L's talking to himself is not a symptom of psychosis, but his physical complaint is; write a report and refer him to the doctor.
   C. There is nothing wrong with L; and since he has not requested medical attention, he should be left alone.
   D. Write a report on his complaints and refer him to the doctor. He may not be psychotic, but his medical complaint should be referred.

5. Prisoner V is charged with petty theft. Apparently, he absent-mindedly walked out of a store with a pair of gloves. Now he claims that he is innocent because he had money to pay for the gloves. Furthermore, he says that he has a bank account with ten thousand dollars. The other prisoners laugh at him, which only makes him angry. Since he has no money and no family, he has not called anyone. Now he wants an attorney and wants to call the largest bank in town for a release of funds.
What should the officer do?

   A. It is obvious that V is senile. He demonstrated this by forgetting he had the gloves when he left the store. Refer to the doctor.
   B. V is hallucinating; he certainly does not behave as though he has money. Refuse him permission to call the bank and refer to the doctor.
   C. Have V give his account number or other method of identifying himself and call the bank. If he has no account, refer to the doctor.
   D. None of the above

6. Officer Y has been watching Prisoner O for the last few days because he felt that O was acting strange. He finally sent a referral memo to the jail administrator that contained the following information: *Prisoner O has been acting strangely the last few days. He seems frightened, mumbles to himself, and walks the floor of his cell a lot. I think he should be seen by the doctor.*
Do you think this report contains sufficient information?

   A. *Yes;* it tells the doctor that the prisoner is acting strangely.
   B. *No;* there is not enough information.
   C. *Yes;* even though there is little information, there is enough for a doctor to know that something is wrong with the prisoner.
   D. *No;* there is very little description. It does not describe how the prisoner acts when frightened, how much walking is a lot, or contain any information that might show if the prisoner is talking to himself or hallucinating.

7. Prisoner G is very forgetful; he can't remember simple rules or follow instructions too well. He is a disciplinary problem because he always seems to be involved in some kind of illegal activity. Yesterday, he was caught with a knife. He claimed he was only carrying it for Prisoner B and claimed he did not know it is contraband. G is a youthful appearing 25 years.
What action should be taken?

   A. G is suffering from extreme advanced senility; refer him for a medical exam.
   B. G is a good liar and is only trying to get out of trouble now that he has been caught.
   C. G seems to be mentally deficient. Rather than harsh punishment, he needs to have someone explain rules to him more clearly. He also needs closer supervision.
   D. None of the above

8. Prisoner J appeared normal when he was admitted to the jail two days ago. Now he seems to be ill. He complains of aching muscles, is weak, and has lost his appetite, and is vomiting.
What seems to be his problem and what should the officer do?

   A. Sounds like flu; refer to the doctor.
   B. J is having drug withdrawal symptoms. He should be referred to the doctor, kept isolated from others, and closely supervised.
   C. J is suffering from insulin shock. He should be kept in a cell away from others until he calms down in a few days.
   D. Sounds like nothing. None of the above.

9. A person on drug withdrawal requires special care, including isolation and close supervision because

   A. drug addicts are usually dangerous and should always be housed in maximum security conditions
   B. he needs to be closely supervised to keep him away from drugs
   C. to prevent him from bothering others, to make it easier to control him, provide close supervision in case he attempts to injure himself
   D. all of the above

10. Officer D has on a number of occasions referred to *sex fiends* and how it is necessary to exercise care when around them because they are dangerous.
    Do you agree?

    A. *Yes;* it is not possible to predict just what a sex offender will do.
    B. *No;* sex offenders are not dangerous while in jail, but I wouldn't want to meet one on the street.
    C. *Yes;* anyone who would commit sex crimes must be untrustworthy and dangerous.
    D. *No;* there are all types of sex offenders, and only a few are violent or dangerous.

11. Officer H has worked in the jail for many years. He is rightfully proud of his ability and experience. He claims that he can always spot a homosexual by his walk and feminine behavior.
    Do you think that Officer H is CORRECT?

    A. *Yes;* all hmosexuals walk like girls and act feminine.
    B. *No;* it is not possible to identify a homosexual without interviewing him.
    C. *Yes;* it's very simple. They are usually slim and have delicate features.
    D. *No;* some masculine-appearing men are homosexual, and often slim delicately-built men are not. It is not appearance but behavior that must be examined.

12. Prisoner Y is slim and has a limp-wristed feminine appearance. Prisoner W is husky and aggressive. Y pretty much minds his own business and does his time. W is loud and is trying very hard to become friends with Y. He keeps offering Y cigarettes and candy which Y refuses. What do you suspect is happening?

    A. Nothing; W is just trying to be friendly.
    B. Obviously Y is homosexual and W doesn't seem to realize it.
    C. Y may or may not be a homosexual; his behavior so far does not indicate that he is. W, however, is acting like an aggressive homosexual and trying to get close to Y.
    D. None of the above

13. Indicate whether the following statements are TRUE or FALSE:

    A. Homosexuals can be easily identified.
    B. A person who talks to himself is psychotic.
    C. People who threaten suicide will not attempt it.
    D. People who threaten suicide are just trying to get sympathy.
    E. Young people have a high suicide rate.
    F. The best method of handling a person who threatens suicide is to call his bluff.
    G. Keeping suicide risks isolated from others is the best way to manage them

14. Prisoner K appears sick. His face is flushed, his skin is dry, and his mouth is dry. His breath is noticeably sweet.
What should you do?

    A. Give him some aspirin and permit him to go on sick call.
    B. Give him orange juice or something else with sugar in it because he is having insulin shock.
    C. Call the doctor immediately; he is suffering from inadequate insulin.
    D. Ignore the matter.

14.____

15. Prisoner P complains of not feeling well. He is pale and weak, his skin is moist, and he seems to be quite shaky as though he were intoxicated. P claims he is diabetic and is in need of something with sugar in it to correct this condition.
What would you do?

    A. Check the records and, if they show he is diabetic, call the doctor and ask for instructions.
    B. Ignore him because this is just another way for some prisoners to get something extra to eat.
    C. Give him candy or orange juice; he is showing symptoms of insulin shock. If he does not feel better almost at once, call the doctor.
    D. Give him the back of your hand.

15.____

16. Prisoner J is having a seizure in his cell.
What should the officer do? (Select five.)

    A. Hold him down so that he does not injure himself.
    B. Remove nearby objects so that he does not injure himself.
    C. Sit him up and give him water to drink.
    D. Wait until the seizure is over and then give him his medication.
    E. Loosen clothing around neck and place a padded object between his teeth to prevent his biting his tongue.
    F. Place coat or pillow beneath prisoner's head to prevent injury.
    G. Turn his face to one side.
    H. Notify the doctor immediately.
    I. The doctor should be routinely informed.

16.____

17. Prisoner J has had four seizures in the last hour. You have followed the proper procedure in helping him in each instance.
What do you do NEXT?

    A. Make certain that he is taking his medication.
    B. Restrain him on his bed so that he does not injure himself during the next seizure.
    C. Call the doctor immediately in order to provide emergency care.
    D. All of the above

17.____

18. As a result of a seizure, Prisoner J has received a head injury. The wound located above the right ear is bleeding. In addition, there seems to be watery fluid flowing from his nose. His breathing is slow and difficult. As yet, he has not regained consciousness as he usually does immediately after a seizure.
What should you do?

    A. Let him sleep; he must be tired from the seizure.
    B. Apply a pressure bandage to stop the bleeding.
    C. Call the doctor; there seems to be evidence that he may have a serious head wound.
    D. Call the warden.
    E. Nothing; he's trying to divert your attention.

18.____

19. The jail officer's responsibility in managing special prisoners includes the following areas: (Select four.)

    A. Diagnosing prisoners' physical and mental condition and referring to the doctor.
    B. Giving first aid whenever it is needed.
    C. Noticing strange or unusual behavior and referring to the doctor.
    D. Developing the ability to describe the physical and emotional condition of prisoners objectively.
    E. Prepare records that describe prisoners' injuries and record their medical complaints.
    F. Evaluate prisoner medical complaints, prescribe medication when required, and keep the chronic complainers from sick call.
    G. Closely supervise the taking of medication, keep careful records of all medicine distributed to and taken by prisoners.

19.____

## KEY (CORRECT ANSWERS)

1. B
2. B
3. A
4. D
5. C

6. D
7. C
8. B
9. C
10. D

11. D
12. C
13. A. F
    B. F
    C. F
    D. F
    E. T
    F. F
    G. F
14. C
15. C
16. B, E, F, G, I
17. C
18. C
19. C, D, E, G

# EXAMINATION SECTION

# TEST 1

DIRECTIONS: Each question or incomplete statement is followed by several suggested answers or completions. Select the one that BEST answers the question or completes the statement. *PRINT THE LETTER OF THE CORRECT ANSWER IN THE SPACE AT THE RIGHT.*

1. You answer a phone complaint from a person concerning an improper labeling practice in a shop in his neighborhood. Upon listening to the complaint, you get the impression that the person is exaggerating and may be too excited to view the matter clearly.
   Of the following, your BEST course would be to
   A. tell the man that you can understand his anger but think it is not a really serious problem
   B. suggest to the man that he file a complaint with the Department of Consumer Affairs
   C. tell the man to stay away from the shop and have his friends do the same
   D. take down the information that the man offers so that he will see that the Police Department is concerned

2. Suppose that late at night you receive a call on 911. The caller turns out to be an elderly man who is not able to get out much and who is calling you not because he needs help but because he wants to talk with someone.
   The BEST way to handle such a situation is to
   A. explain to him that the number is for emergencies and his call may prevent others from getting the help they need
   B. talk to him if not many calls are coming in but excuse yourself and cut him off if you are busy
   C. cut him off immediately when you find out he does not need help because this will be the most effective way of discouraging him
   D. suggest that he call train or bus information as the clerks there are often not busy at night

3. While you are on duty, you receive a call from a person whose name your recognize to be that of a person who calls frequently about matters of no importance. The caller requests your name and your supervisor's name so that she can report you for being impolite to her.
   You should
   A. ask her when and how you were impolite to her
   B. tell her that she should not call about such minor matters
   C. make a report about her complaint for your superior
   D. give her the information that she requests

4. Of the following, the MOST important reason for requiring each employ of the Police Department to be responsible for good public relations is that
   A. the Police Department has better morale when employees join in an effort to improve public relations
   B. the public judges the Department according to impressions received at every level in the Department
   C. most employees will not behave well toward the public unless required to do so
   D. employees who improve public relations will receive commendations from superiors

5. Assume that you are in the Bureau of Public Relations. You receive a telephone call from a citizen who asks if a study has been made of the advisability of combining the city's police and fire departments. Assume that you have no information on the subject.
   Of the following, your BEST course would be to
   A. tell the caller that undoubtedly the subject has been studied but that you do not have the information available
   B. suggest to the caller that he telephone the Fire Department's Community Relations section for further information
   C. explain to the caller that the functions of the two departments are distinct and that combining them would be inefficient
   D. take the caller's number in order to call back, and then find information or referrals to give him

6. Suppose that Police Department officials have discouraged representatives of the press from contacting police administrative aides (except aides in the Public Relations Bureau) for information.
   Of the following, the BEST reason for such a policy would be to
   A. assure proper control over information released to the press by the Department
   B. increase the value of official press releases of the Department
   C. make press representatives realize that the Department is not seeking publicity
   D. reduce the chance of crimes being committed in imitation of those reported in the press

7. People who phone the Police Department often use excited, emotional, and sometimes angry speech.
   The BEST policy for you to take when speaking to this type of caller is to
   A. tell the person directly that he must speak in a more civil way
   B. tell the caller to call back when he is in a better mood
   C. give the person time to settle down, by doing most of the talking yourself
   D. speak calmly yourself to help the caller to gradually become more relaxed

8. On a particularly busy evening, the police administrative aide assigned to the telephones had answered a tremendous number of inquiries and complaints by irate citizens. His patience was exhausted when he received a call from a citizen who reported, *Officer, a bird just flew into my bedroom. What should I do?* In a release of tension, the aide responded, *Keep it for seven days; and if no one claims it, it is yours.*
   This response by the aide would usually be considered
   A. *advisable*, because the person should see how unusual his question was
   B. *advisable*, because he avoided offering police services that were unavailable
   C. *not advisable*, because such a remark might be regarded as insulting rather than humorous
   D. *not advisable*, because the person might not want a bird for a pet

9. While temporarily assigned to switchboard duty, you receive a call from a man who says his uncle in Pittsburgh has just called him and threatened to commit suicide. The man is convinced his uncle intends to carry out his threat.
   Of the following, you should
   A. advise the man to have neighbors of the uncle check to see if the uncle is all right
   B. politely inform the man that such out-of-town incidents are beyond the authority of the local precinct
   C. take the uncle's name, address, and telephone number and immediately contact police authorities in Pittsburgh
   D. get the man's name, address, and telephone number so that you can determine whether the call is a hoax

10. Assume that in the course of your assigned duties you have just taken a necessary action which you feel has angered a citizen. After he has gone, you suddenly realize that the incident might result in an unjustified complaint.
    The MOST advisable action for you to take now would be to
    A. contact the person and apologize to him
    B. make complete notes on the incident and on any witnesses who might be helpful
    C. ask your superior what you might expect in case of such a complaint, without giving any hint of the actual occurrence
    D. accept the situation as one of the hazards of your job

11. Your job may bring you in contact with people from the community who are confronted with emergencies,, and are experiencing feelings of tension, anxiety, or even hostility. It is good to keep in mind what attitude is most helpful to people who, in such situations like these.
    Which of the following would be BEST to do?
    A. Present similar examples of your own problems to make the person feel that his problems are not unusual.
    B. Recognize the person's feelings, present information on available services, and make suggestions as to proper procedures

C. Expect that some of the information is exaggerated and encourage the person to let some time pass before seeking further help.
D. Have the person wait while you try to make arrangements for his problem to be solved.

12. Suppose that while on duty you receive a call from the owner of a gas station which is located within the precinct. The owner is annoyed with a certain rule made by the Police Department which concerns the operation of such stations. You agree with him.
Of the following, the BEST action for you to take is to
   A. make a report on the call and suggest to the owner that he write a letter to the Department about the rule
   B. tell the owner that there is little that can be done since such rules are departmental policy
   C. tell the owner that you agree with his complaint and that you will write a memo of his call
   D. establish good relations with the owner by suggesting how to word a letter that will get action from the department

12.____

13. Suppose that you are working at the switchboard when a call comes in late at night from a woman who reports that her neighbors are having a very noisy party. She gives you her first name, surname, and address, and you ask her title is *Miss* or *Mrs.* She replies that her title is irrelevant to her complaint, and wants to know why you ask.
Of the following possible ways of handling this, which is BEST?
   A. Insist that the title is necessary for identification purposes
   B. Tell her that it is merely to find out what her marital status is
   C. Agree that the information is not necessary and ask her how she wants to be referred to
   D. Find out why she shows such a peculiar reaction to a request for harmless information

13.____

14. While covering an assignment on the switchboard, you receive a call from a young girl who tells you of rumored plans for a gang fight in her neighborhood. You should
   A. take down the information so that a patrol squad can investigate the area and possibly keep the fight from starting
   B. discourage the girl from becoming alarmed by reminding her that it is only a rumor
   C. realize that this is a teenager looking for attention, humor her, and dismiss the matter
   D. take down the information but tell the girl that you need concrete information, and not just rumors, to take any action on her call

14.____

15. The one of the following which would MOST likely lead to friction among police administrative aides in a unit would be for the supervisor in charge of the unit to
   A. defend the actions of the aides he supervises when discussing them with his own supervisor

15.____

B. get his men to work together as a team in completing the work of the unit
C. praise each of the aides he supervises *in confidence* as the best aide in the unit
D. consider the point of view of the aides he supervises when assigning unpleasant tasks

16. Suppose that a police administrative aide who had been transferred to your office from another unit in your Department because of difficulties with his supervisor has been placed under your supervision.
    The BEST course of action for you to take FIRST is to
    A. analyze the aide's past grievance to determine if the transfer was the best settlement of the problem
    B. advise him of the difficulties his former supervisor had with other employees and encourage him not to feel bad about the transfer
    C. warn him that you will not tolerate any nonsense and that he will be watched carefully while assigned to your unit
    D. instruct him in the duties he will be performing in your unit and make him feel *wanted* in his new position

17. In which of the following circumstances would it be MOST appropriate for you to use an impersonal style of writing rather than a personal style, which relies on the use of personal pronouns and other personal references?
    When writing a memorandum to
    A. give your opinion to an associate on the advisability of holding a weekly staff meeting
    B. furnish your superior with data justifying a proposed outlay of funds for new equipment
    C. give your version of an incident which resulted in a complaint by a citizen about your behavior
    D. support your request for a transfer to another division

18. A newly appointed supervisor should learn as much as possible about the backgrounds of his subordinates.
    The statement is generally CORRECT because
    A. effective handling of subordinates is based upon knowledge of their individual differences
    B. knowing their backgrounds assures they will be treated objectively, equally, and without favor
    C. some subordinates perform more efficiently under one supervisor than under another
    D. subordinates have confidence in a supervisor who knows all about them

19. You have found it necessary, for valid reasons, to criticize the work of one of the female police administrative aides. She later comes to your desk and accuses you of criticizing her work because she is a woman.
    The BEST way for you to deal with this employee is to
    A. ask her to apologize, since you would never allow yourself to be guilty of his kind of discrimination

B. discuss her complaint with her, explaining again and at greater length the reason for your criticism
C. assure her you wish to be fair, and ask her to submit a written report to you on her complaint
D. apologize for hurting her feelings and promise that she will be left alone in the future

20. The following steps are recognized steps in teaching an employee a new skill:
    I. Demonstrate how to do the work
    II. Let the learner do the work himself
    III. Explain the nature and purpose of the work
    IV. Correct poor procedures by suggestion and demonstration
    The CORRECT order for these steps is
      A. III, II, IV, I   B. II, I, III, IV   C. III, I, II, IV   D. I, III, II, IV

21. Suppose you have arranged an interview with a subordinate to try to help him overcome a serious shortcoming in his technical work. While you do not intend to talk to him about his attitude, you have noticed that he seems to be suspicious and resentful of people in authority. You need a record of the points covered in the discussion since further interviews are likely to be necessary.
    Your BEST course would be to
      A. write a checklist of points you wish to discuss and carefully check the points off as the interview progresses
      B. know exactly how you wish to proceed, and then make written notes during the interview of your subordinate's comments
      C. frankly tell your subordinate that you are recording the talk on tape but place the recorder where it will not hinder discussion
      D. keep in mind what you wish to accomplish and make notes on the interview immediately after it is over

22. A police administrative aide has explained a complicated procedure to several subordinates. He has been talking clearly, allowing time for information to sink in. He has also encouraged questions. Yet, he still questions his subordinates after his explanation, with the obvious objective of finding out whether they completely understand the procedure.
    Under these circumstances, the action of the police administrative aide, in asking questions about the procedure, is
      A. *not advisable*, because subordinates who do not now know the procedure which has been explained so carefully can read and study it
      B. *not advisable*, because he endangers his relationship with his subordinates by insulting their intelligence
      C. *advisable*, because subordinate basically resent instructions and seldom give their full attention in a group situation
      D. *advisable*, because the answers to his questions help him to determine whether he has gained his objective

23. The most competent of the police administrative aides is a pleasant, intelligent young woman who breaks the rules of the Department by occasionally making long personal telephone calls during working hours. You have not talked to her up until now about this fault. However, the calls are beginning to increase, and you decide to deal directly with the problem.
The BEST way to approach the subject with her would be to
    A. review with her the history of her infractions of the rules
    B. point out that her conduct is not fair to the other workers
    C. tell her that her personal calls are excessive and discuss it with her
    D. warn her quietly that you intend to apply penalties if necessary

23._____

24. Assume that you are supervising eight male police administrative aides who do similar clerical work. A group of four of them work on each side of a row of files which can be moved without much trouble. You notice that in each group there is a clique of three aides, leaving one member isolated. The two isolated members are relative newcomers.
Your BEST course in such a case would be to
    A. ignore the situation because to concern yourself with informal social arrangements of your subordinates would distract you from more important matters
    B. ask each of the cliques to invite the isolated member in their working group to lunch with them from time to time
    C. tell each group that you cannot allow cliques to form as it is bad for the morale of the unit
    D. find an excuse to move the file cabinet to the side of the room and then move the desks of the two isolated members close together

24._____

25. Suppose that your supervisor, who has recently been promoted and transferred to your division, asks you to review a certain procedure with a view to its possible revision. You know that several years ago a sergeant made a lengthy and intensive report based on a similar review.
Which of the following would it be BEST for you to do FIRST?
    A. Ask your supervisor if he is aware of the previous report
    B. Read the sergeant's report before you begin work to see what bearing it has on your assignment
    C. Begin work on the review without reading his report so that you will have a fresh point of view
    D. Ask the sergeant to assist you in your review

25._____

26. Using form letters in business correspondence is LEAST effective when
    A. answering letters on a frequently recurring subject
    B. giving the same information to many addresses
    C. the recipient is only interested in the routing information contained in the form letter
    D. a reply must be keyed to the individual requirements of the intended reader

26._____

27. From the viewpoint of an office administrator, the BEST of the following reasons for distributing the incoming mail before the beginning of the regular work day is that
    A. distribution can be handled quickly and most efficiently at that time
    B. distribution later in the day may be distracting to or interfering with other employees
    C. the employees who distribute the mail can then perform other tasks during the rest of the day
    D. office activities for the day based on the mail may then be started promptly

28. Suppose you have had difficulty locating a document in the files because you could not decide where it should have been filed. You learn that other people in the office have had the same problem. You know that the document will be needed from time to time in the future.
    Your BEST course, when refiling the document, would be to
    A. make a written note of where you found it so that you will find it more easily the next time
    B. reclassify it and file it in the file where you first looked for it
    C. file it where you found it and put cross-reference sheets in the other likely files
    D. make a mental association to help you find it the next time and put it back where you found it

29. Suppose that your supervisor is attending a series of meetings of police captains in Philadelphia and will not be back until next Wednesday. He has left no instructions with you as to how you should handle telephone calls for him.
    In most instances, your BEST course of action would be to say:
    A. He isn't here just now.
    B. He is out of town and won't be back until next Wednesday.
    C. He won't be in today.
    D. He is in Philadelphia attending a meeting of police captains.

30. The one of the following which is USUALLY an important by-product of the preparation of a procedure manual is that
    A. information uncovered in the process of preparation may lead to improvement of procedures
    B. workers refer to the manual instead of bothering their supervisors for information
    C. supervisors use the manual for training stenographers
    D. employees have equal access to information needed to do their jobs

31. You have been asked to organize a clerical job and supervise police administrative aides who will do the actual work. The job consists of removing, from several boxes of data processing cards which are arranged in alphabetical order, the cards of those whose names appear on certain lists. The person removing the card then notes a date on the card. Assume that the work will be done accurately whatever system is used.

Which of the following statements describes both the MOST efficient method and the BEST reasons for using that method?  Have
  A. two aides work together, one calling names and the other extracting cards, and dating them, because the average production of any two aides working together should be higher, under these circumstances, than that of any two aides working alone
  B. each aide work alone, because it is easier to check spelling when reading the names than when listening to them
  C. two aides work together, one calling names and the other extracting cards and dating them, because social interaction tends to make work go faster
  D. each aide work alone, because the average production of any two aides, each working alone, should be higher, under these circumstances, than that of any two aides working together

32. The term *work flow*, when used in connection with office management or the activities in an office GENERALLY means the    32.____
  A. rate of speed at which work flows through a single section of an office
  B. use of charts in the analysis of various office functions
  C. number of individual work units which can be produced by the average employee
  D. step-by-step physical routing of work through its various procedures

Questions 33-40.

DIRECTIONS:  Name of Offense       V A N D S B R U G H
             Code Letter           c o m p l e x i t y
             File Number           1 2 3 4 5 6 7 8 9 0

Assume that each of the above capital letters is the first letter of the name of an offense, that the small letter directly beneath each capita letter is the code letter for the offense, and that the number directly beneath each code letter is the file number for the offense.
In each of Questions 33 through 40, the code letters and file numbers should correspond to the capital letters.
If there is an error only in Column 2, mark your answer A.
If there is an error only in Column 3, mark your answer B.
If there is an error in both Column 2 and Column, mark your answer C.
If both Columns 2 and 3 are correct, mark your answer D.
Sample Questions:
| COLUMN 1 | COLUMN 2 | COLUMN 3 |
| --- | --- | --- |
| BNARGHSVVU | emoxtylcci | 6357905118 |

The code letters in Column 2 are correct, but the first 5 in Column 3 should be 2.  Therefore, the answer is B.

| | COLUMN 1 | COLUMN 2 | COLUMN 3 | |
| --- | --- | --- | --- | --- |
| 33. | HGDSBNBSVR | ytplxmelcx | 0945736517 | 33._____ |

| | | | | |
|---|---|---|---|---|
| 34. | SDGUUNHVAH | lptiimycoy | 5498830120 | 34.____ |
| 35. | BRSNAAVUDU | exlmooctpi | 6753221848 | 35.____ |
| 36. | VSRUDNADUS | cleipmopil | 1568432485 | 36.____ |
| 37. | NDSHVRBUAG | mplycxeiot | 3450175829 | 37.____ |
| 38. | GHUSNVBRDA | tyilmcexpo | 9805316742 | 38.____ |
| 39. | DBSHVURANG | pesycixomt | 4650187239 | 39.____ |
| 40. | RHNNASBDGU | xymnolepti | 7033256398 | 40.____ |

## KEY (CORRECT ANSWERS)

| | | | | | | | |
|---|---|---|---|---|---|---|---|
| 1. | B | 11. | B | 21. | D | 31. | D |
| 2. | A | 12. | A | 22. | D | 32. | D |
| 3. | D | 13. | C | 23. | C | 33. | C |
| 4. | B | 14. | A | 24. | D | 34. | D |
| 5. | D | 15. | C | 25. | A | 35. | A |
| 6. | A | 16. | D | 26. | D | 36. | C |
| 7. | D | 17. | B | 27. | D | 37. | B |
| 8. | C | 18. | A | 28. | C | 38. | D |
| 9. | C | 19. | B | 29. | B | 39. | A |
| 10. | B | 20. | C | 30. | A | 40. | C |

# EXAMINATION SECTION
## TEST 1

DIRECTIONS: Each question or incomplete statement is followed by several suggested answers or completions. Select the one that BEST answers the question or completes the statement. *PRINT THE LETTER OF THE CORRECT ANSWER IN THE SPACE AT THE RIGHT.*

Questions 1-8.

DIRECTIONS: Each of Questions 1 through 8 consists of a statement which contains a word (one of those underlined) that is either incorrectly used because it is not in keeping with the meaning the quotation is evidently intended to convey or is misspelled. There is only one INCORRECT word in each quotation. Of the four underlined words, determine if the first one should be replaced by the word lettered A, the second replaced by the word lettered B, the third replaced by the word lettered C, or the fourth replaced by the word lettered D. Print the letter of the replacement word you have selected in the space at the right.

1. Whether one depends on fluorescent or artificial light or both, adequate standards should be maintained by means of systematic tests.
   A. natural    B. safeguards    C. established    D. routine

1.____

2. An officer has to be prepared to assume his knowledge as a social scientist in the community.
   A. forced    B. role    C. philosopher    D. street

2.____

3. It is practically impossible to indicate whether a sentence is too long simply by measuring its length.
   A. almost    B. tell    C. very    D. guessing

3.____

4. Strong leaders are required to organize a community for delinquency prevention and for dissemination of organized crime and drug addiction.
   A. tactics    B. important    C. control    D. meetings

4.____

5. The demonstrators, who were taken to the Criminal Courts building in Manhattan (because it was large enough to accommodate them), contended that the arrests were unwarrented.
   A. exhibitors    B. legions    C. adjudicate    D. unwarranted

5.____

6. The were guaranteed a calm atmosphere, free from harassment, which would be conducive to quiet consideration of the indictments.
   A. guaranteed    B. atmospher    C. harassment    D. inditements

6.____

7. The alleged killer was occasionally permitted to excercise in the corridor.
   A. alledged    B. ocasionally    C. permited    D. exercise

7.____

8. Defense counsel stated, in affect, that their conduct was permissable under the First Amendment.
   A. council   B. effect   C. there   D. permissable

8.____

Questions 9-12.

DIRECTIONS: Each of the two sentences in Questions 9 through 12 may be correct or may contain errors in punctuation, capitalization, or grammar. If there is an error only in sentence I, mark your answer A. If there is an error in both sentence I and sentence II, mark your answer C. If both sentence I and sentence II are correct, mark your answer D.

9. I. It is very annoying to have a pencil sharpener, which is not in working order.
   II. Officer Blake checked the door of Joe's Restaurant and found that the lock has been jammed.

9.____

10. I. When you are studying a good textbook is important.
    II. He said he would divide the money equally between you and me.

10.____

11. I. Since he went on the city council a year ago, one of his primary concerns has been safety in the streets.
    II. After waiting in the doorway for about 15 minutes, a black sedan appeared.

11.____

12. I. The question is, "What is the difference between a lawful and an unlawful demonstration?"
    II. The captain assigned two detectives, John and I, to the investigation.

12.____

Questions 13-14.

DIRECTIONS: In each of Questions 13 and 14, the four sentences are from a paragraph in a report. They are not in the right order. Which of the following arrangement is the BEST one?

13. I. Most organizations favor one of the types but always include the others to a lesser degree.
    II. However, we can detect a definite trend toward greater use of symbolic control.
    III. We suggest that our local police agencies are today primarily utilizing material control.
    IV. Control can be classified into three types: physical, material, and symbolic.
    The CORRECT answer is:
    A. IV, II III, I   B. II, I, IV, III   C. III, IV, II, I   D. IV, I, III, II

13.____

14. I They can and do take advantage of ancient political and geographical boundaries, which often give them sanctuary from effective policy activity.
    II. This country is essentially a country of small police forces, each operating independently within the limits of its jurisdiction.

14.____

III. The boundaries that define and limit police operations do not hinder the movement of criminals, of course.
IV. The machinery of law enforcement in America is fragmented, complicated, and frequently overlapping.

The CORRECT answer is
A. III, I, II, IV      B. II, IV, I, III      C. IV, II, III, I      D. IV, III, II, I

15. Generally, the frequency with which reports are to be submitted or the length of the interval which they cover should depend MAINLY on the
A. amount of time needed to prepare the reports
B. degree of comprehensiveness required in the reports
C. availability of the data to be included in the reports
D. extent of the variations in the data with the passage of time

16. Suppose you have to write a report on a serious infraction of rules by one of the police administrative aides you supervise. The circumstances in which the infraction occurred are quite complicated.
The BEST way to organize this report would be to
A. give all points equal emphasis throughout the report
B. include more than one point in a paragraph only if necessary to equalize the size of paragraphs
C. place the least important points before the most important points
D. present each significant point in a separate paragraph

17. Suppose that police expenses in the city in a certain year amounted to 7.5% of total expenses.
In indicating this percentage on a *pie* or circular chart, which is 360, the size of the angle between the two radiuses would be MOST NEARLY
A. 3.7      B. 7.5      C. 27      D. 54

18. Suppose that in police precinct A, where there are 4,180 children, 627 children entered a contest sponsored by the Police Community Relations Bureau. In precinct B, where there were 7,840 children, 1,960 children entered the contest.
The total percentage of all children in both precincts who entered the contest amounted to MOST NEARLY
A. 19.5%      B. 20%      C. 21.5%      D. 22.5%

19. If Circle A represents Police Administrative Aides (PAA's) who scored above 85 on a PAA test and Circle B represents PAA's who scored above 85 on a Senior PAA test, then the diagram at the right means that
A. no PAA who scored above 85 on a PAA test scored above 85 on the Senior PAA test
B. the majority of PAA's who scored above 85 on a PAA test scored above 85 on the Senior PAA test
C. there were some PAA's who did not take the Senior PAA test
D. some PAA's who scored above 85 on a PAA test scored above 85 on the Senior PAA test

20. Suppose that in 1912 the city had a population of 550,000 and a police force of 200, and that in 2012 the city had a population of 8,000,000 and a police force of 32,000.
If the ratio of police to population in 2012 is compared with the same ratio in 1912, what is the resulting relationship of the 2012 ratio to the 1912 ratio?
A. 160:11  B. 160:1  C. 16:1  D. 11:1

Questions 21-24.

DIRECTIONS: Questions 21 through 24 are to be answered SOLELY on the basis of the information contained in the following passage.

Of those arrested in the city in 2019 for felonies or misdemeanors, only 32% were found guilty of any charge. Fifty-six percent of such arrestees were acquitted or had their cases dismissed, 11% failed to appear for trial, and 1% received other dispositions. Of those found guilty, only 7.4% received any sentences of over one year in jail. Only 50% of those found guilty were sentenced to any further time in jail. When considered with the low probability of arrests for most crimes, these figures make it clear that the crime control system in the city poses little threat to the average criminal. Delay compounds the problem. The average case took four appearances for disposition after arraignment. Twenty percent of all cases took eight or more appearances to reach a disposition. Forty-four percent of all cases took more than one year to disposition.

21. According to the above passage, crime statistics for 2019 indicate that
    A. there is a low probability of arrests for all crimes in the city
    B. the average criminal has much to fear from the law in the city
    C. over 10% of arrestees in the city charged with felonies or misdemeanors did not show up for trial
    D. criminals in the city are less likely to be caught than criminals in the rest f the country

22. The percentage of those arrested in 2019 who received sentences of over one year in jail amounted MOST NEARLY to
    A. .237  B. 2.4  C. 23.7  D. 24.0

23. According to the above passage, the percentage of arrestees in 2019 who were found guilty was
    A  20% of those arrested for misdemeanors
    B. 11% of those arrested for felonies
    C. 50% of those sentenced to further time in jail
    D. 32% of those arrested for felonies or misdemeanors

24. According to the above passage, the number of appearances after arraignment and before disposition amounted to
    A. an average of four
    B. eight or more in 44% of the cases
    C. over four for cases which took more than a year
    D. between four and eight for most cases

Questions 25-27.

DIRECTIONS: Questions 25 through 27 are to be answered SOLELY on the basis of the information contained in the following passage.

The traditional characteristics of a police organization, which do not foster group-centered leadership, are being changed daily by progressive police administrators. These characteristics are authoritarian and result in a leader-centered style with all determination of policy and procedure made by the leader. In the group-centered style, policies and procedures are a matter for group discussion and decision. The supposedly modern view is that the group-centered style is the most conducive to improving organizational effectiveness. By contrast, the traditional view regards the group-centered style as an idealistic notion of psychologists. It is questionable, however, that the situation determines the appropriate leadership style. In some circumstances, it will be leader-centered; in others, group-centered. Nevertheless, police supervisors will see more situations calling for a leadership style that, while flexible, is primarily group-centered. Thus, the supervisor in a police department must have a capacity not just to issue orders but to engage in behavior involving organizational leadership which primarily emphasizes goals and work facilitation.

25. According to the above passage, there is reason to believe that with regard to the effectiveness of different types of leadership, the
    A. leader-centered type is better than the individual-centered type or the group-centered type
    B. leader-centered type is best in some situations and the group-centered type best in other situations
    C. group-centered type is better than the leader-centered type in all situations
    D. authoritarian type is least effective in democratic countries

26. According to the above passage, police administrators today are
    A. more likely than in the past to favor making decisions on the basis of discussions with subordinates
    B. likely in general to favor traditional patterns of leadership in their organizations
    C. more likely to be progressive than conservative
    D. practical and individualistic rather than idealistic in their approach to police problems

27. According to the above passage, the role of the police department is changing in such a way that its supervisors must
    A. give greater consideration to the needs of individual subordinates
    B. be more flexible in dealing with infractions of department rules
    C. provide leadership which stresses the goals of the department and helps the staff to reach them
    D. refrain from issuing orders and allow subordinates to decide how to carry out their assignments

Questions 28-31.

DIRECTIONS: Questions 28 through 31 are to be answered SOLELY on the basis of the information contained in the following passage.

Under the provisions of the Bank Protection Act of 1968, enacted July 8, 1968, each Federal banking supervisory agency, as of January 7, 1969, had to issue rules establishing minimum standards with which financial institutions under their control must comply with respect to the installation, maintenance, and operation of security devices and procedures, reasonable in cost, to discourage robberies, burglaries, and larcenies, and to assist in the identification and apprehension of persons who commit such acts. The rules set the time limits within which the affected banks and savings and loan associations must comply with the standards, and the rules require the submission of periodic reports on the steps taken. A violator of a rule under this Act is subject to a civil penalty not to exceed $100 for each day of the violation. The enforcement of these regulations rests with the responsible banking supervisory agencies.

28. The Bank Protection Act of 1968 was designed to
    A. provide Federal police protection for banks covered by the Act
    B. have organizations covered by the Act take precautions against criminals
    C. set up a system for reporting all bank robberies to the FBI
    D. insure institutions covered by the Act from financial loss due to robberies, burglaries, and larcenies

29. Under the provisions of the Bank Protection Act of 1968, each Federal banking supervisory agency was required to set up rules for financial institutions covered by the Act governing the
    A. hiring of personnel
    B. punishment of burglars
    C. taking of protective measures
    D. penalties for violations

30. Financial institutions covered by the Bank Protection Act of 1968 were required to
    A. file reports at regular intervals on what they had done to prevent theft
    B. identify and apprehend persons who commit robberies, burglaries, and larcenies
    C. draw up a code of ethics for their employees
    D. have fingerprints of their employees filed with the FBI

31. Under the provisions of the Bank Protection Act of 1968, a bank which is subject to the rules established under the Act and which violates a rule is liable to a penalty of NOT _____ than $100 for each _____.
    A. more; violation
    B. less; day of violation
    C. less; violation
    D. more; day of violation

Questions 32-36.

DIRECTIONS: Questions 32 through 36 are to be answered SOLELY on the basis of the information contained in the following passage.

A statement which is offered in an attempt to prove the truth of the matters therein stated, but which is not made by the author as a witness before the court at the particular trial in which it is so offered, is hearsay. This is so whether the statement consists of words (oral or written), of symbols used as a substitute for words, or of signs or other conduct offered as the equivalent of a statement. Subject to some well-established exceptions, hearsay is not generally acceptable as evidence, and it does not become competent evidence just because it is received by the court without objection. One basis for this rule is simply that a fact cannot be proved by showing that somebody stated it was a fact. Another basis for the rule is the fundamental principle that in a criminal prosecution the testimony of the witness shall be taken before the court, so that at the time he gives the testimony offered in evidence he will be sworn and subject to cross-examination, the scrutiny of the court, and confrontation by the accused.

32. Which of the following is hearsay? A(n)
    A. written statement by a person not present at the court hearing where the statement is submitted as proof of an occurrence
    B. oral statement in court by a witness of what he saw
    C. written statement of what he saw by a witness present in court
    D. re-enactment by a witness in court of what he saw

33. In a criminal case, a statement by a person not present in court is
    A. *acceptable* evidence if not objected to by the prosecutor
    B. *acceptable* evidence if not objected to by the defense lawyer
    C. *not acceptable* evidence except in certain well-settled circumstances
    D. *not acceptable* evidence under any circumstances

34. The rule on hearsay is founded on the belief that
    A. proving someone said an act occurred is not proof that the act did occur
    B. a person who has knowledge about a case should be willing to appear in court
    C. persons not present in court are likely to be unreliable witnesses
    D. permitting persons to testify without appearing in court will lead to a disrespect for law

35. One reason for the general rule that a witness in a criminal case must give his testimony in court is that
    A. a witness may be influenced by threats to make untrue statements
    B. the opposite side is then permitted to question him
    C. the court provides protection for a witness against unfair questioning
    D. the adversary system is designed to prevent a miscarriage of justice

36. Of the following, the MOST appropriate title for the above passage would be
    A. What is Hearsay           B. Rights of Defendants
    C. Trial procedures          D. Testimony of Witnesses

Questions 37-40.

DIRECTIONS: Questions 37 through 40 are to be answered SOLELY on the basis of the following graphs.

8 (#1)

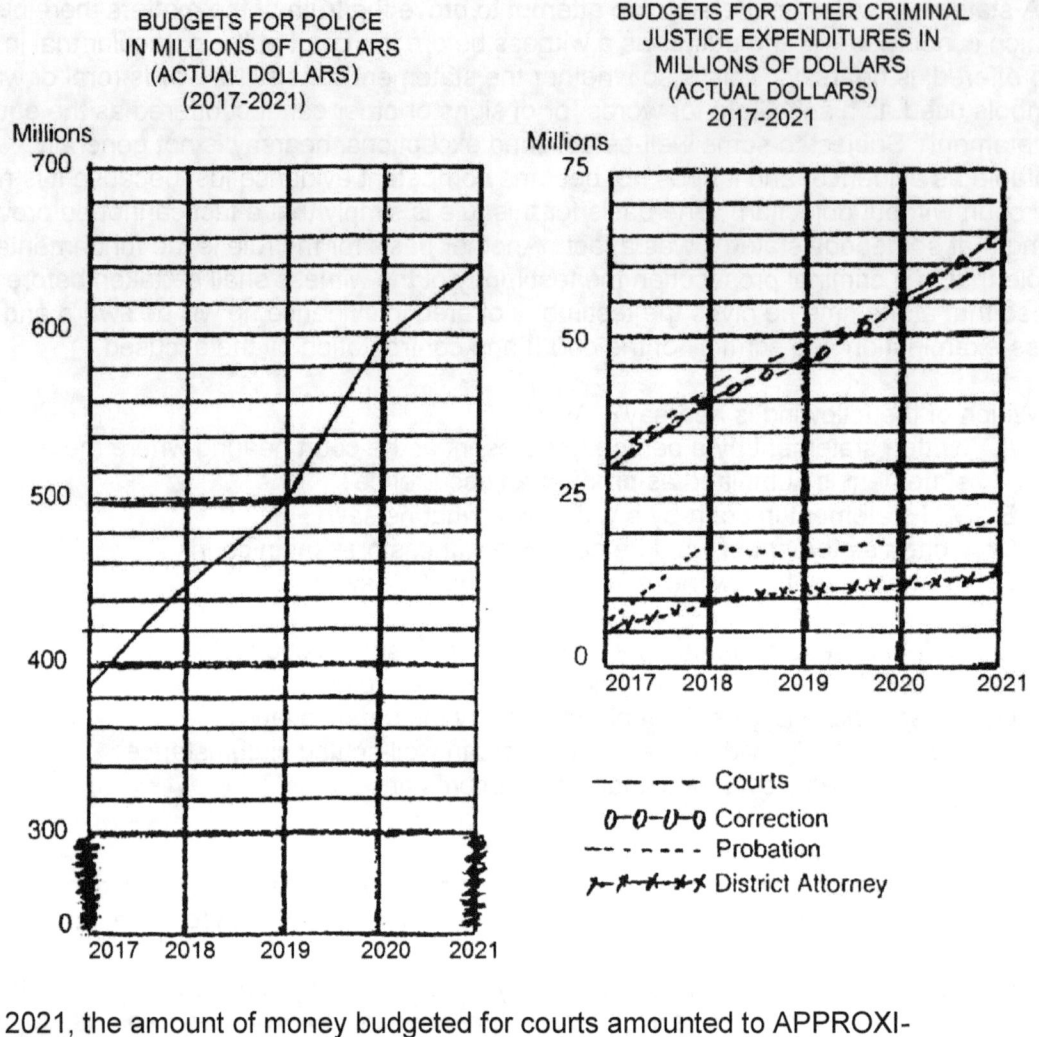

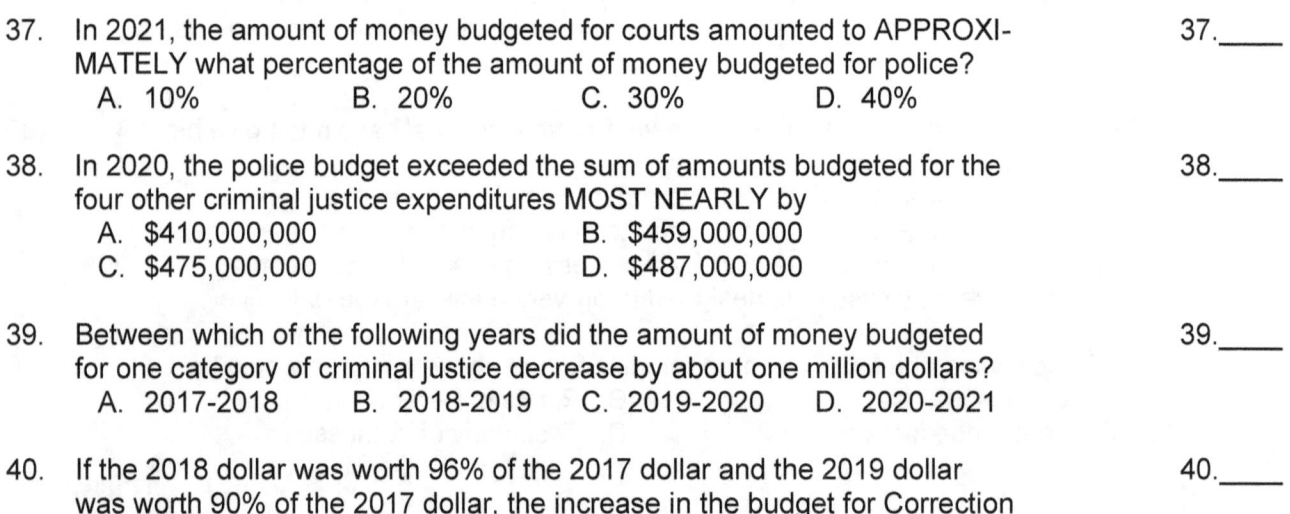

37. In 2021, the amount of money budgeted for courts amounted to APPROXI-    37.____
MATELY what percentage of the amount of money budgeted for police?
   A. 10%         B. 20%         C. 30%         D. 40%

38. In 2020, the police budget exceeded the sum of amounts budgeted for the    38.____
four other criminal justice expenditures MOST NEARLY by
   A. $410,000,000                B. $459,000,000
   C. $475,000,000                D. $487,000,000

39. Between which of the following years did the amount of money budgeted    39.____
for one category of criminal justice decrease by about one million dollars?
   A. 2017-2018    B. 2018-2019    C. 2019-2020    D. 2020-2021

40. If the 2018 dollar was worth 96% of the 2017 dollar and the 2019 dollar    40.____
was worth 90% of the 2017 dollar, the increase in the budget for Correction
from 2018 to 2019, in terms of the 2017 dollar, amounted to
   A. $2,100,000    B. $4,200,000    C. $4,320,ooo    D. $4,700,000

## KEY (CORRECT ANSWERS)

| | | | | | | | |
|---|---|---|---|---|---|---|---|
| 1. | A | 11. | C | 21. | C | 31. | D |
| 2. | B | 12. | B | 22. | B | 32. | A |
| 3. | B | 13. | D | 23. | D | 33. | C |
| 4. | C | 14. | C | 24. | A | 34. | A |
| 5. | D | 15. | D | 25. | B | 35. | B |
| 6. | C | 16. | D | 26. | A | 36. | A |
| 7. | D | 17. | C | 27. | C | 37. | A |
| 8. | B | 18. | C | 28. | B | 38. | B |
| 9. | C | 19. | D | 29. | C | 39. | B |
| 10. | A | 20. | D | 30. | A | 40. | A |

# EXAMINATION SECTION
# TEST 1

DIRECTIONS: Each question or incomplete statement is followed by several suggested answers or completions. Select the one that BEST answers the question or completes the statement. *PRINT THE LETTER OF THE CORRECT ANSWER IN THE SPACE AT THE RIGHT.*

1. You and a co-worker have been given a rush job to classify 50 sets of fingerprints. Although you started out with 25 sets each, the ones you were given were less complicated; and when you are finished, your co-worker still has several sets to work on. It would be BEST for you to

    A. go back to your normal assignment
    B. offer to help your co-worker with the work he has left
    C. recheck the work you have done since you have extra time
    D. wait until your co-worker is finished before turning in your work, so it doesn't look as though he was *goofing off*

2. Several prospective police department employees arrive to be fingerprinted. One of the people arrives a few minutes later than the others but insists he must be fingerprinted first since he has important personal business to attend to. In addition, he is insolent and impolite. It would be BEST for you to

    A. fingerprint this person first so he will stop bothering you
    B. politely explain to this person that he must wait his turn
    C. refuse to fingerprint the person until he apologizes to you
    D. write a memo to the personnel office stating that you think this person should not be hired

3. While you are filing a fingerprint card, you notice another card that is misfiled. It would be BEST for you to

    A. ask your co-workers why the card is in the wrong place
    B. leave the card where it is since someone may have a good reason for putting it there
    C. remove the card from the drawer and refile it in the correct place
    D. send the card to your supervisor with a note explaining that you found it misfiled

4. You receive a telephone call from someone claiming to be a police officer who asks you for information about the criminal record of another person. This information might be in the files you have access to. The BEST thing for you to do would be to

    A. ask him to write you a letter requesting the information
    B. check the files and give him the information if you have it
    C. explain to him that such requests must be made through the office handling such records
    D. tell him you do not have the information

5. Assume your supervisor gives you a group of fingerprinting cards to file. In glancing over them, you notice they have not been classified as most cards are before they are filed. The BEST thing you can do in this situation is

A. ask a technician to classify the fingerprints and then file them
B. file the cards anyway, since that is what you were told to do
C. leave the cards on your desk until your supervisor asks you whether you filed them; then explain why you did not do so
D. point out the omission to your supervisor before you file the cards

6. You are filing a large stack of fingerprint cards when a newly hired probationary patrolman arrives at your office to be fingerprinted before starting work. For you to finish your filing before fingerprinting him would be

   A. *correct;* if you stop in the middle of your filing, you may make mistakes when you return to it
   B. *incorrect;* the patrolman might overhear confidential information while waiting for you
   C. *correct;* you should not start to fingerprint someone until you can devote your full attention to the job
   D. *incorrect;* it is not good practice to keep someone waiting while you do paperwork which could be done later

7. Your supervisor gives you a rush job alphabetizing a stack of fingerprint cards. You start the job, but are distracted by a conversation with a fellow employee and forget to finish the work. When your supervisor asks you for the completed work, the BEST thing for you to tell him would be that you

   A. did not understand his instructions
   B. forgot to finish the job but will do it as soon as you can
   C. have been working steadily on the job but have not had time to finish it
   D. were given a more important assignment

8. Your office has only one telephone line which is sometimes used to call a technician or trainee for rush work. You must make a lengthy personal telephone call during working hours. For you to make the call on the office telephone would be

   A. *proper;* employees must occasionally handle personal matters during working hours
   B. *improper;* a rush call could be delayed while you have the phone tied up
   C. *proper;* you should not leave the office to make personal calls during working hours
   D. *improper;* other people in the office might overhear your personal business

9. While using the fingerprint files, you find a card for one of your neighbors. The card indicates that many years earlier the person was convicted of attempted murder, though your neighbor has told you he was arrested for the crime but never convicted. The BEST thing for you to do would be to

   A. accuse your neighbor of lying to you about his past
   B. change the card so that it indicates arrest without conviction
   C. say nothing to anyone about this police record
   D. tell your neighbor the police have an incorrect record for him

10. You have been instructed that a technician or trainee must be available in the fingerprint unit for rush work. On a certain day your co-workers are out of the office at lunch time. The BEST thing for you to do would be to

A. ask a clerk from another office to cover your office while you go out to lunch
B. lock the office and take your lunch hour
C. put off your lunch hour until a technician or trainee returns
D. take a quick break for lunch and handle any rush work when you return

11. If a secretary who has never worked in the fingerprint unit returns some fingerprint cards that his supervisor has borrowed, the BEST way to have the cards refiled accurately would be to   11._____

    A. explain the filing system to him so that he can re-file them himself
    B. have him refile them and check his work later
    C. refile them yourself when you have a chance
    D. tell him his supervisor is responsible for refiling borrowed cards

12. After you have been working for a short time, you think you have developed a system which will make the filing of fingerprint cards more efficient. The BEST thing for you to do would be to   12._____

    A. ask your co-workers to try the new method for a few days to see if it really works
    B. describe the new method to your supervisor and ask her if she thinks it would help
    C. say nothing about your idea since it has probably been tried unsuccessfully by someone else
    D. use the new method yourself but say nothing to anyone else since they might resent your interference

13. The MOST appropriate statement for Mr. Jones to make when answering the telephone in his office is:   13._____

    A. Fingerprint Unit, Mr. Jones speaking
    B. Good morning, Fingerprint Unit
    C. Hello, who is this?
    D. May I help you?

14. The work space used by any clerk should be well organized. In order to work efficiently, it is MOST important that the worker's desk be arranged so that   14._____

    A. materials needed for work are within easy reach
    B. personal belongings do not take up any drawer space
    C. it is neat in appearance
    D. the top of the desk is clear of all papers

15. When you arrive at work one day, you find a note from your supervisor with instructions for a special assignment she wants you to perform. However, you do not understand certain of the instructions. It would be BEST for you to   15._____

    A. carry out the instructions the way you think they should be done
    B. find your supervisor and ask her to clarify the instructions
    C. show the note to your co-workers and ask them what they think you should do
    D. tell your supervisor, when she asks you for the completed assignment, that you have not done the work because you did not understand the instructions

16. In most offices some workers gossip about other people there. With regard to such gossip, a new employee in the fingerprint unit should   16._____

A. be interested in any information he can learn about his co-workers
B. discuss the information with the supervisor in order to learn the truth
C. pass the information on to those workers who would be interested in the news
D. try to ignore the information since there is usually little truth to it

17. Closing file drawers immediately after use is important MAINLY because it

A. is a safety precaution
B. is otherwise possible to file material in the wrong file drawer
C. makes it possible for other workers to use adjoining file drawers
D. protects the tabs on the file folders from ripping

18. The FIRST step in filing cards alphabetically is to

A. count the cards
B. divide the cards into groups of ten
C. inspect each card to insure that it is filled out completely
D. rearrange the cards in alphabetical order

19. If you cannot find the folder on Michael Hillston in an alphabetic file, you should

A. assume that the folder is lost
B. check other places where the folder could easily have been misfiled, like Hilston and Hillson
C. look through all of the alphabetic files to see whether the folder was misplaced
D. return to your other work and check for the folder again the next day

20. Of the following, the type of filing system used in the MOST efficiently run office depends MOSTLY on the

A. way records are used or requested
B. geographical location of the office
C. skill of clerical personnel who do the filing
D. number of filing clerks employed

21. The MOST important reason for well-organized files is to insure that

A. business papers and records can easily be found
B. company documents will be arranged alphabetically
C. file space will be efficiently utilized for business purposes
D. it is possible to identify the individual who committed any errors

Questions 22-26.

DIRECTIONS: Questions 22 through 26 are to be answered based on an alphabetical arrangement of the following list of names.

| Walker, Carol J. | Wacht, Michael | Wade, Ethel |
| Wall, Fredrick | Wall, Francis | Wall, Frank |
| Wachs, Paul | Walker, Carol L. | Wagner, Arthur |
| Walters, Daniel | Wade, Ellen | Wald, William |
| Wagner, Allen | Walters, David | Walker, Carmen |

22. The 4th name on the alphabetized list would be 22.____
    A. Wade, Ellen   B. Wade, Ethel
    C. Wagner, Allen   D. Wagner, Arthur

23. The 7th name on the alphabetized list would be 23.____
    A. Walker, Carmen   B. Walker, Carol J.
    C. Walker, Carol L.   D. Wald, William

24. The name that would come immediately AFTER Wagner, Arthur on the alphabetized list would be 24.____
    A. Wade, Ethel   B. Wagner, Allen
    C. Wald, William   D. Walker, Carol L.

25. The name that would come immediately BEFORE Wall, Frank would be 25.____
    A. Wall, Francis   B. Wall, Fredrick
    C. Walters, David   D. Walters, Daniel

26. The 12th name on the alphabetized list would be 26.____
    A. Walker, Carol L.   B. Wald, William
    C. Wall, Francis   D. Wall, Frank

Questions 27-35.

DIRECTIONS: Questions 27 through 35 are to be answered SOLELY on the basis of the following information and the following list of individuals and identification numbers.

Assume that the police department is planning to conduct a statistical study of individuals who have been convicted of crimes during a certain year. For the purpose of this study, identification numbers are being assigned to individuals in the following manner:

The first two digits indicate the age of the individual. The third digit indicates the sex of the individual:
   1. male
   2. female
The fourth digit indicates the type of crime involved:
   1. criminal homicide
   2. forcible rape
   3. robbery
   4. aggravated assault
   5. burglary
   6. larceny
   7. auto theft
   8. other

The fifth and sixth digits indicate the month in which the conviction occurred:
   01. January
   02. February, etc.

| | | | |
|---|---|---|---|
| Abbott, Richard | 271304 | Morris, Chris | 212705 |
| Collins, Terry | 352111 | Owens, William | 231412 |

| | | | |
|---|---|---|---|
| Elders, Edward | 191207 | Parker, Leonard | 291807 |
| George, Linda | 182809 | Robinson, Charles | 311102 |
| Hill Leslie | 251702 | Sands, Jean | 202610 |
| Jones, Jackie | 301106 | Smith, Michael | 421308 |
| Lewis, Edith | 402406 | Turner, Donald | 191601 |
| Mack, Helen | 332509 | White, Barbara | 242803 |

27. The number of women on the above list is

    A. 6　　　B. 7　　　C. 8　　　D. 9

28. The two convictions which occurred during February were for the crimes of

    A. aggravated assault and auto theft
    B. auto theft and criminal homicide
    C. burglary and larceny
    D. forcible rape and robbery

29. The ONLY man convicted of auto theft was

    A. Richard Abbott　　　B. Leslie Hill
    C. Chris Morris　　　D. Leonard Parker

30. The number of people on the list who were 25 years old or older is

    A. 6　　　B. 7　　　C. 8　　　D. 9

31. The OLDEST person on the list is

    A. Terry Collins　　　B. Edith Lewis
    C. Helen Mack　　　D. Michael Smith

32. The two people on the list who are the same age are

    A. Richard Abbott and Michael Smith
    B. Edward Elders and Donald Turner
    C. Linda George and Helen Mack
    D. Leslie Hill and Charles Robinson

33. A 28-year-old man who was convicted of aggravated assault in October would have identification number

    A. 281410　　　B. 281509　　　C. 282311　　　D. 282409

34. A 33-year-old woman convicted in April of criminal homicide would have identification number

    A. 331140　　　B. 331204　　　C. 332014　　　D. 332104

35. The number of people on the above list who were convicted during the first six months of the year is

    A. 6　　　B. 7　　　C. 8　　　D. 9

Questions 36-45.

DIRECTIONS: Questions 36 through 45 test how good you are at catching mistakes in typing or printing. In each question, the name and address in Column II should be an exact copy of the name and address in Column I. Mark your answer:
- A. if there is no mistake in either name or address
- B. if there are mistakes in both name and address
- C. if there is a mistake only in the name
- D. if there is a mistake only in the address.

| COLUMN I | COLUMN II | |
|---|---|---|
| 36. Arturo Rodriguez<br>2156 Cruger Avenue<br>Bronx, New York 10446 | Arturo Rodrigues<br>2156 Cruger Avenue<br>Bronx, New York 10446 | 36.____ |
| 37. Helen McCabe<br>2044 East 19 Street<br>Brooklyn, New York 11204 | Helen McCabe<br>2040 East 19 Street<br>Brooklyn, New York 11204 | 37.____ |
| 38. Charles Martin<br>526 West 160 Street<br>New York, N.Y. 10022 | Charles Martin<br>526 West 160 Street<br>New York, N.Y. 10022 | 38.____ |
| 39. Morris Rabinowitz<br>31 Avenue M<br>Brooklyn, N.Y. 11216 | Morris Rabinowitz<br>31 Avenue N<br>Brooklyn, N.Y. 11216 | 39.____ |
| 40. Joseph DiSilva<br>63-84 Saunders Road<br>Rego Park, N.Y. 11431 | Joseph Disilva<br>64-83 Saunders Road<br>Rego Park, N.Y. 11431 | 40.____ |
| 41. Linda Polansky<br>2225 Fenton Avenue<br>Bronx, N.Y. 10464 | Linda Polansky<br>2255 Fenton Avenue<br>Bronx, N.Y. 10464 | 41.____ |
| 42. Alfred Klein<br>260 Hillside Terrace<br>Staten Island, N.Y. 15545 | Alfred Klein<br>260 Hillside Terrace<br>Staten Island, N.Y. 15545 | 42.____ |
| 43. William McDonnell<br>504 E. 55 Street<br>New York, N.Y. 10103 | William McConnell<br>504 E. 55 Street<br>New York, N.Y. 10108 | 43.____ |
| 44. Angela Cipolla<br>41-11 Parsons Avenue<br>Flushing, N.Y. 11446 | Angela Cipola<br>41-11 Parsons Avenue<br>Flushing, N.Y. 11446 | 44.____ |
| 45. Julie Sheridan<br>1212 Ocean Avenue<br>Brooklyn, N.Y. 11237 | Julia Sheridan<br>1212 Ocean Avenue<br>Brooklyn, N.Y. 11237 | 45.____ |

# KEY (CORRECT ANSWERS)

| | | | | |
|---|---|---|---|---|
| 1. B | 11. C | 21. A | 31. D | 41. D |
| 2. B | 12. B | 22. B | 32. B | 42. A |
| 3. C | 13. A | 23. D | 33. A | 43. B |
| 4. C | 14. A | 24. C | 34. D | 44. C |
| 5. D | 15. B | 25. A | 35. C | 45. C |
| 6. D | 16. D | 26. D | 36. C | |
| 7. B | 17. A | 27. B | 37. D | |
| 8. B | 18. D | 28. B | 38. A | |
| 9. C | 19. B | 29. B | 39. D | |
| 10. C | 20. A | 30. D | 40. B | |

# TEST 2

DIRECTIONS: Each question or incomplete statement is followed by several suggested answers or completions. Select the one that BEST answers the question or completes the statement. *PRINT THE LETTER OF THE CORRECT ANSWER IN THE SPACE AT THE RIGHT.*

Questions 1-10.

DIRECTIONS: Questions 1 through 10 are to be answered ONLY on the basis of the following information.
Column I consists of identification numbers of fingerprints.
Column II shows different ways of arranging the corresponding identification numbers.

The identification numbers of the fingerprints in Column I begin and end with a capital letter and have an eight-digit number in between. The identification numbers in Column I are to be arranged according to the following rules:

1. In alphabetical order according to the first letter.
2. When two or more identification numbers have the same first letter, in alphabetical order according to the last letter.
3. When two or more identification numbers have the same first AND last letters, in numerical order, beginning with the lowest number.

The identification numbers in Column I are numbered 1 through 5. In Column II, the numbers 1 through 5 are arranged in four different ways to show different arrangements of the corresponding identification numbers. Choose the answer in Column II in which the identification numbers are arranged according to the above rules.

SAMPLE QUESTION

COLUMN I
(1) E75044127B
(2) B96399104A
(3) B93939086A
(4) B47064465H
(5) B99040922A

COLUMN II
A. 4, 1, 3, 2, 5
B. 4, 1, 2, 3, 5
C. 4, 3, 2, 5, 1
D. 3, 2, 5, 4, 1

In the sample question, the four identification numbers starting with B should be put before the identification number starting with E. The identification numbers starting with B and ending with A should be put before the identification number starting with B and ending with M. The three identification numbers starting with B and ending with A should be listed in numerical order, beginning with the lowest number. The CORRECT way to arrange the identification numbers, therefore, is:

(3) B93939086A
(2) B96399104A
(5) B99040922A
(4) B47064465H
(1) E75044127B

2 (#2)

Since the order of arrangement is 3, 2, 5, 4, 1, the answer to the sample question is D.

COLUMN I                COLUMN II

1. (1) B33886897B        A. 5, 1, 3, 4, 2        1.____
   (2) B38386882B        B. 1, 2, 5, 3, 4
   (3) D33389862B        C. 1, 2, 5, 4, 3
   (4) D33336887D        D. 2, 1, 4, 5, 3
   (5) B38888697D

2. (1) E11664554M        A. 4, 1, 2, 5, 3        2.____
   (2) F11164544M        B. 2, 4, 1, 5, 3
   (3) F11614455N        C. 4, 2, 1, 3, 5
   (4) E11665454M        D. 1, 4, 2, 3, 5
   (5) F16161545N

3. (1) C86611355W        A. 2, 4, 1, 5, 3        3.____
   (2) C68631533V        B. 1, 2, 4, 3, 5
   (3) G88633331W        C. 1, 2, 5, 4, 3
   (4) C68833515V        D. 1, 2, 4, 3, 5
   (5) G68833511W

4. (1) R73665312J        A. 3, 2, 1, 4, 5        4.____
   (2) P73685512J        B. 2, 3, 5, 1, 4
   (3) P73968511J        C. 2, 3, 1, 5, 4
   (4) R73665321K        D. 3, 1, 5, 2, 4
   (5) R63985211K

5. (1) X33661222U        A. 1, 4, 5, 2, 3        5.____
   (2) Y83961323V        B. 4, 5, 1, 3, 2
   (3) Y88991123V        C. 4, 5, 1, 2, 3
   (4) X33691233U        D. 4, 1, 5, 2, 3
   (5) X38691333U

6. (1) B22838847W        A. 4, 5, 2, 3, 1        6.____
   (2) B28833874V        B. 4, 2, 5, 1, 3
   (3) B22288344X        C. 4, 5, 2, 1, 3
   (4) B28238374V        D. 4, 1, 5, 2, 3
   (5) B28883347V

7. (1) H44477447G        A. 1, 3, 5, 4, 2        7.____
   (2) H47444777G        B. 3, 1, 5, 2, 4
   (3) H74777477C        C. 1, 4, 2, 3, 5
   (4) H44747447G        D. 3, 5, 1, 4, 2
   (5) H77747447C

8. (1) G11143447G        A. 3, 5, 1, 4, 2        8.____
   (2) G15133388C        B. 1, 4, 3, 2, 5
   (3) C15134378G        C. 5, 3, 4, 2, 1
   (4) G11534477C        D. 4, 3, 1, 2, 5
   (5) C15533337C

68

9.  (1) J96693369F
    (2) J66939339F
    (3) J96693693E
    (4) J96663933E
    (5) J69639363F

    A. 4, 3, 2, 5, 1
    B. 2, 5, 4, 1, 3
    C. 2, 5, 4, 3, 1
    D. 3, 4, 5, 2, 1

    9._____

10. (1) L15567834Z
    (2) P11587638Z
    (3) M51567688Z
    (4) O55578784Z
    (5) N53588783Z

    A. 3, 1, 5, 2, 4
    B. 1, 3, 5, 4, 2
    C. 1, 3, 5, 2, 4
    D. 3, 1, 5, 4, 2

    10._____

Questions 11-17.

DIRECTIONS: Each of Questions 11 through 17 consists of a long series of letters and numbers under Column I and four short series of letters and numbers under Column II. For each question, choose the short series of letters and numbers which is entirely and exactly the same as some part of the long series.

SAMPLE QUESTION

COLUMN I
JG13572XY89WB14

COLUMN II
A. 1372Y8
B. XYWB14
C. 72XY89
D. J13572

In each of choices A, B, and D, one or more of the letters and numbers in the series in Column I is omitted. Only option C reproduces a segment of the series entirely and exactly. Therefore, C is the CORRECT answer to the sample question.

COLUMN I

11. P473R365M442V5W

    COLUMN II
    A. P47365
    B. 73P365
    C. 365M44
    D. 5X42V5

    11._____

12. 865CG441V21SS59

    A. 1V12SS
    B. V21SS5
    C. 5GC441
    D. 894CG4

    12._____

13. 1E227FE383L4700

    A. E27FE3
    B. EF838L
    C. EL4700
    D. 83L470

    13._____

14. 77J646G54NPB318

    A. NPB318
    B. J646J5
    C. 4G54NP
    D. C54NPB

    14._____

15. 85887T358W24A93
 A. 858887
 B. W24A93
 C. 858W24
 D. 87T353

16. E104RY796B33H14
 A. 04RY79
 B. E14RYR
 C. 96B3H1
 D. RY7996

17. W58NP12141DE07M
 A. 8MP121
 B. W53NP1
 C. 14DE07
 D. 12141D

Questions 18-27

DIRECTIONS: Questions 18 through 27 are to be answered on the basis of the following information.

The phonetic filing system is a method of filing names in which the alphabet is reduced to key code letters. The six key letters and their equivalents are as follows:

| KEY LETTERS | EQUIVALENTS |
| --- | --- |
| b | p, f, v |
| c | s, k, g, j, q, x, z |
| d | t |
| l | none |
| m | n |
| r | none |

A key letter represents itself.
Vowels (a, e, i, o, and u) and the letters w, h, and y are omitted.
For example, the name GILMAN would be represented as follows:

G is represented by the key letter c
I is a vowel and is omitted
L is a key letter and represents itself
M is a key letter and represents itself
A is a vowel and is omitted
N is represented by the key letter M

Therefore, the phonetic filing code for the name GILMAN is CLMM.

18. The phonetic filing code for the name FITZGERALD would be
 A. BDCCRLD   B. BDCRLD   C. BDZCRLD   D. BTZCRLD

19. The phonetic filing code CLBR may represent any one of the following names EXCEPT
 A. Calprey   B. Flower   C. Glover   D. Silver

20. The phonetic filing code LDM may represent any one of the following names EXCEPT    20.____

    A. Halden        B. Hilton        C. Walton        D. Wilson

21. The phonetic filing code for the name RODRIGUEZ would be    21.____

    A. RDRC          B. RDRCC         C. RDRCZ         D. RTRCC

22. The phonetic filing code for the name MAXWELL would be    22.____

    A. MCLL          B. MCWL          C. MCWLL         D. MXLL

23. The phonetic filing code for the name ANDERSON would be    23.____

    A. AMDRCM        B. ENDRSM        C. MDRCM         D. NDERCN

24. The phonetic filing code for the name SAVITSKY would be    24.____

    A. CBDCC         B. CBDCY         C. SBDCC         D. SVDCC

25. The phonetic filing code CMC may represent any one of the following names EXCEPT    25.____

    A. James         B. Jayes         C. Johns         D. Jones

26. The ONLY one of the following names that could be represented by the phonetic filing code CDDDM would be    26.____

    A. Catalano                       B. Chesterton
    C. Cittadino                      D. Cuttlerman

27. The ONLY one of the following names that could be represented by the phonetic filing code LLMCM would be    27.____

    A. Ellington                      B. Hallerman
    C. Inslerman                      D. Willingham

Questions 28-35.

DIRECTIONS: Questions 28 through 35 test how well you compare figures. Each question shows figures that have a certain feature in common. Mark the letter of the choice that also has that feature.

28.    28.____

6 (#2)

29.

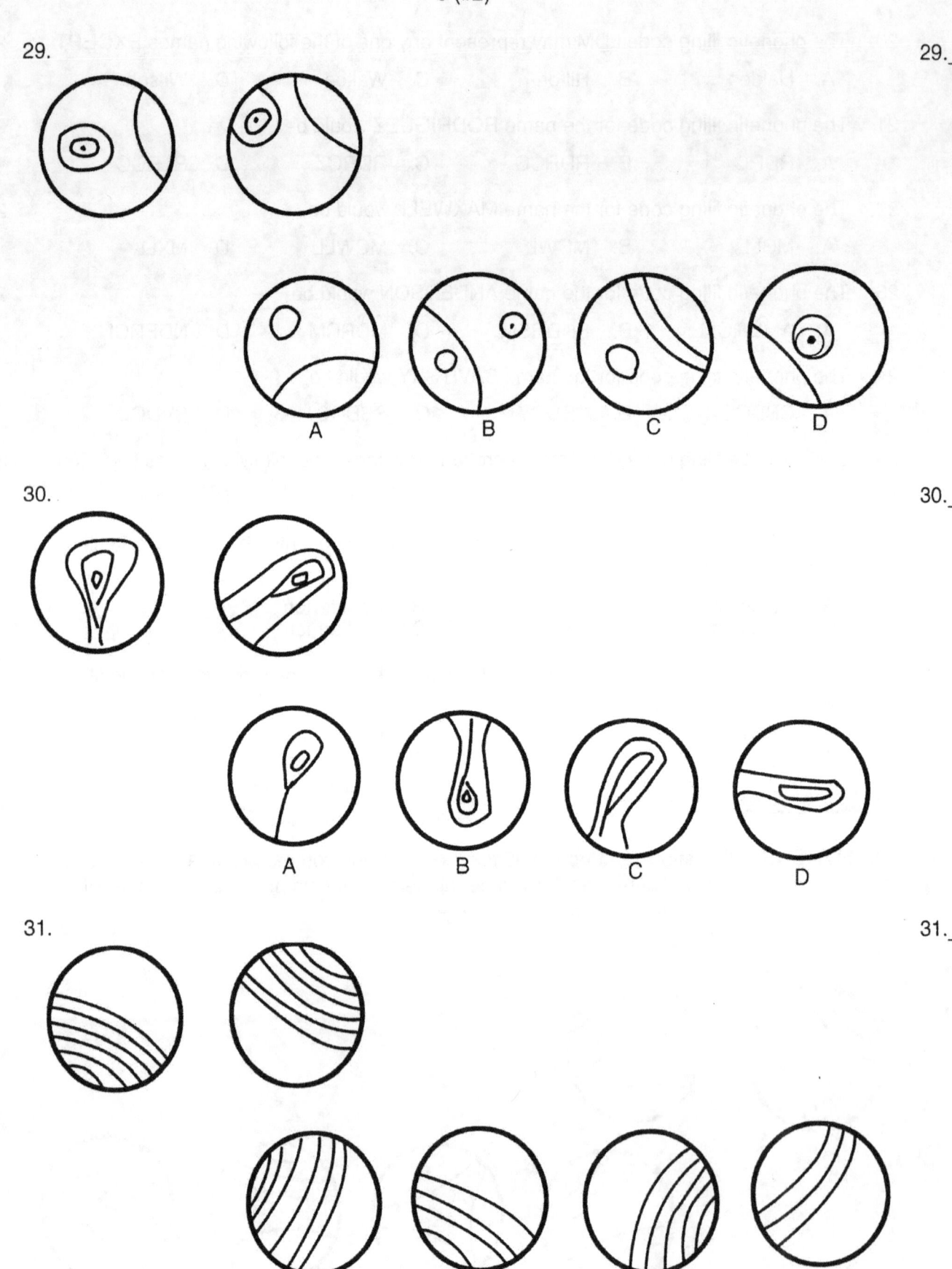

30.

31.

32.

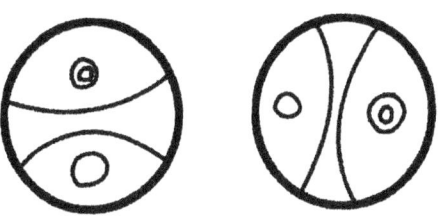

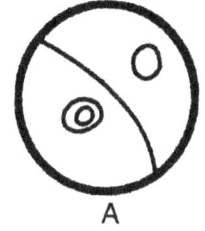 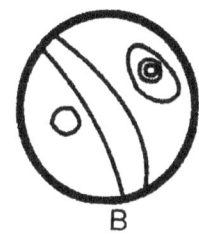 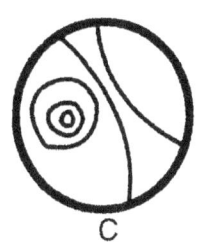 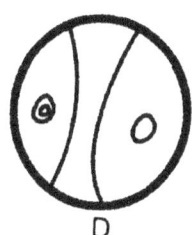
A　　　　　　B　　　　　　C　　　　　　D

33.

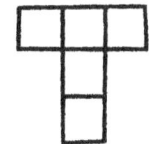 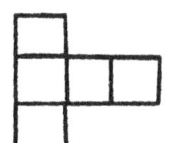

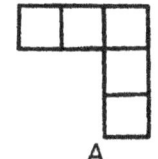 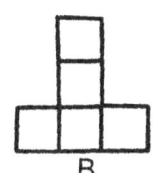 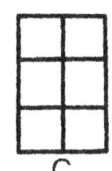 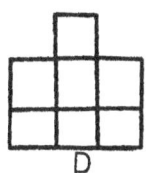
A　　　　　　B　　　　　　C　　　　　　D

34.

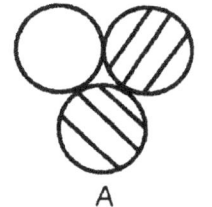 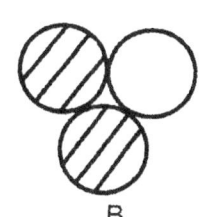 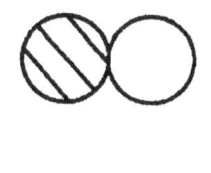 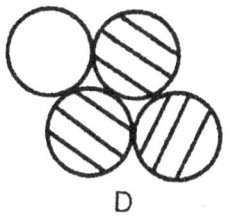
A　　　　　　B　　　　　　C　　　　　　D

35.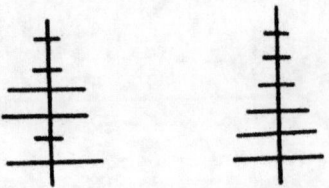

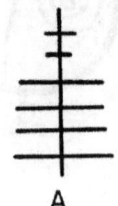 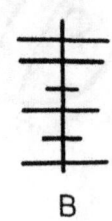 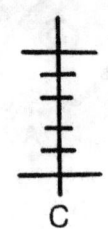 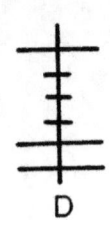
A       B       C       D

---

## KEY (CORRECT ANSWERS)

1. B
2. D
3. A
4. C
5. A

6. B
7. D
8. C
9. A
10. B

11. C
12. B
13. D
14. A
15. B

16. A
17. D
18. A
19. B
20. D

21. B
22. A
23. C
24. A
25. B

26. C
27. D
28. C
29. D
30. B

31. A
32. D
33. B
34. A
35. D

---

# ARITHMETIC
# EXAMINATION SECTION
# TEST 1

DIRECTIONS: Each question or incomplete statement is followed by several suggested answers or completions. Select the one that *BEST* answers the question or completes the statement. *PRINT THE LETTER OF TEE CORRECT ANSWER IN THE SPACE AT THE RIGHT.*

1. Add $4.34, $34.50, $6.00, $101.76, $90.67. From the result, subtract $60.54 and $10,56.  1.____
   A. $76.17   B. $156.37   C. $166.17   D. $300.37

2. Add 2,200, 2,600, 252 and 47.96. From the result, subtract 202.70, 1,200, 2,150 and 434.43.  2.____
   A. 1,112.83   B. 1,213.46   C. 1,341.51   D. 1,348.91

3. Multiply 1850 by .05 and multiply 3300 by .08 and, then, add both results,  3.____
   A. 242.50   B. 264,00   C. 333.25   D. 356.50

4. Multiply 312.77 by .04. Round off the result to the nearest hundredth.  4.____
   A. 12.52   B. 12.511   C. 12.518   D. 12.51

5. Add 362.05, 91.13, 347.81 and 17.46 and then divide the result by 6. The answer, rounded off to the nearest hundredth, is:  5.____
   A. 138.409   B. 137.409   C. 136.41   D. 136.40

6. Add 66.25 and 15.06 and, then, multiply the result by 2 1/6.
   The answer is, most nearly,  6.____
   A. 176.18   B. 176.17   C. 162.66   D. 162.62

7. Each of the following items contains three decimals. In which case do *all* three decimals have the *SAME* value?  7.____
   A. .3; .30; .03           B. .25; .250; .2500
   C. 1.9; 1.90;1.09         D. .35; .350; .035

8. Add 1/2 the sum of (539.84 and 479.26) to 1/3 the sum of (1461.93 and 927.27). Round off the result to the nearest whole number.  8.____
   A. 3408   B. 2899   C. 1816   D. 1306

9. Multiply $5,906.09 by 15% and, then, divide the result by 3 and round off to the nearest cent.  9.____
   A. $295.30   B. $885.91   C. $2,657.74   D. $29,530.45

10. Multiply 630 by 517.  10.____
    A. 325,710   B. 345,720   C. 362,425   D. 385,660

11. Multiply 35 by 846.

    A. 4050    B. 9450    C. 18740    D. 29610

11._____

12. Multiply 823 by 0.05.

    A. 0.4115    B. 4.115    C. 41.15    D. 411.50

12._____

13. Multiply 1690 by 0.10.

    A. 0.169    B. .1.69    C. 16.90    D. 169.0

13._____

14. Divide 2765 by 35.

    A. 71    B. 79    C. 87    D. 93

14._____

15. From $18.55 subtract $6.80.

    A. $9.75    B. $10.95    C. $11.75    D. $25.35

15._____

16. The sum of 2.75 + 4.50 + 3.60 is:

    A. 9.75    B. 10.85    C. 11.15    D. 11.95

16._____

17. The sum of 9.63 + 11.21 + 17.25 is:

    A. 36.09    B. 38.09    C. 39.92    D. 41.22

17._____

18. The sum of 112.0 + 16.9 + 3.84 is:

    A. 129.3    B. 132.74    C. 136.48    D. 167.3

18._____

19. When 65 is added to the result of 14 multiplied by 13, the answer is:

    A. 92    B. 182    C. 247    D. 16055

19._____

20. From $391.55 subtract $273.45.

    A. $118.10    B. $128.20    C. $178.10    D. $218.20

20._____

## KEY (CORRECT ANSWERS)

1. C        11. D
2. A        12. C
3. D        13. D
4. D        14. B
5. C        15. C

6. B        16. B
7. B        17. B
8. D        18. B
9. C        19. C
10. A       20. A

## SOLUTIONS TO PROBLEMS

1. ($4.34 + $34.50 + $6.00 + $101.76 + $90.67) - ($60.54 + $10.56) = $237.27 - $71.10 = $166.17.

2. (2200 + 2600 + 252 + 47.96) - (202.70 + 1200 + 2150 + 434.43) = 5099.96 - 3987.13 = 1112.83

3. (1850)(.05) + (3300)(.08) = 92.5 + 264 = 356.50

4. (312.77)(.04) = 12.5108 = 12.51 to nearest hundredth

5. $(362.05 + 91.13 + 347.81 + 17.46) \div 6 = 136.40\overline{83} = 136.41$ to nearest hundredth

6. $(66.25 + 15.06)(2\frac{1}{6}) = 176.17\overline{16} \approx 176.17$

7. .25 = .250 = .2500

8. $(\frac{1}{2})(539.84 + 479.26) + \frac{1}{3}(1461.93 + 927.27) = 509.55 + 796.4 = 1305.95 = 1306$ nearest whole number

9. ($5906.09)(.15) ÷ 3 = ($885.9135)/3 = 295.3045 = $295.30 to nearest cent

10. (630)(517) = 325,710

11. (35)(846) = 29,610

12. (823)(.05) = 41.15

13. (1690)(10) = 169.0

14. 2765 ÷ 3.5 = 79

15. $18.55 - $6.80 = $11.75

16. 2.75 + 4.50 + 3.60 = 10.85

17. 9.63 + 11.21 + 17.25 = 38.09

18. 112.0 + 16.9 + 3.84 = 132.74

19. 65 + (14)(13) = 65 + 182 = 247

20. $391.55 - $273.45 = $118.10

# TEST 2

DIRECTIONS   Each question or incomplete statement is followed by several suggested answers or completions. Select the one that *BEST* answers the question or completes the statement. *PRINT THE LETTER OF TEE CORRECT ANSWER IN THE SPACE AT THE RIGHT.*

1. The sum of $29.61 + $101.53 + $943.64 is:      1.____
   A. $983.88      B. $1074.78      C. $1174.98      D. $1341.42

2. The sum of $132.25 + $85.63 + $7056,44 is:      2.____
   A. $1694.19      B. $7274.32      C. $8464.57      D. $9346.22

3. The sum of 4010 + 1271 + 838 + 23 is:      3.____
   A. 6142      B. 6162      C. 6242      D. 6362

4. The sum of 53632 + 27403 + 98765 + 75424 is:      4.____
   A. 19214      B. 215214      C. 235224      D. 255224

5. The sum of 76342 + 49050 + 21206 + 59989 is:      5.____
   A. 196586      B. 206087      C. 206587      D. 234487

6. The sum of $452.13 + $963.45 + $621.25 is:      6.____
   A. $1936.83      B. $2036.83      C. $2095.73      D. $2135.73

7. The sum of 36392 + 42156 + 98765 is:      7.____
   A. 167214      B. 177203      C. 177313      D. 178213

8. The sum of 40125 + 87123 + 24689 is:      8.____
   A. 141827      B. 151827      C. 151937      D. 161947

9. The sum of 2379 + 4015 + 6521 + 9986 is:      9.____
   A. 22901      B. 22819      C. 21801      D. 21791

10. From 50962 subtract 36197.      10.____
    A. 14675      B. 14765      C. 14865      D. 24765

11. From 90000 subtract 31928.      11.____
    A. 58072      B. 59062      C. 68172      D. 69182

12. From 63764 subtract 21548.      12.____
    A. 42216      B. 43122      C. 45126      D. 85312

13. From $9605.13 subtract $2715.96.      13.____
    A. $12,321.09      B. $8,690.16      C. $6,990.07      D. $6,889.17

14. From 76421 subtract 73101.  14.____
    A. 3642    B. 3540    C. 3320    D. 3242

15. From $8.25 subtract $6.50.  15.____
    A. $1.25   B. $1.50   C. $1.75   D. $2.25

16. Multiply 583 by 0.50.  16.____
    A. $291.50   B. 28.15   C. 2.815   D. 0.2815

17. Multiply 0.35 by 1045.  17.____
    A. 0.36575   B. 3.6575   C. 36.575   D. 365.75

18. Multiply 25 by 2513.  18.____
    A. 62825   B. 62725   C. 60825   D. 52825

19. Multiply 423 by 0.01.  19.____
    A. 0.0423   B. 0.423   C. 4.23   D. 42.3

20. Multiply 6.70 by 3.2.  20.____
    A. 2.1440   B. 21.440   C. 214.40   D. 2144.0

# KEY (CORRECT ANSWERS)

1. B        11. A
2. B        12. A
3. A        13. D
4. D        14. C
5. C        15. C

6. B        16. A
7. C        17. D
8. C        18. A
9. A        19. C
10. B       20. B

3 (#2)

# SOLUTIONS TO PROBLEMS

1. $29.61 + $101.53 + $943.64 = $1074.78

2. $132.25 + $85.63 + $7056.44 = $7274.32

3. 4010 + 1271 + 838 + 23 = 6142

4. 53,632 + 27,403 + 98,765 + 75,424 = 255,224

5. 76,342 + 49,050 + 21,206 + 59,989 = 206,587

6. $452.13 + $963.45 + $621.25 = $2036.83

7. 36,392 + 42,156 + 98,765 = 177,313

8. 40,125 + 87,123 + 24,689 = 151,937

9. 2379 + 4015 + 6521 + 9986 = 22,901

10. 50962 - 36197 = 14,765

11. 90,000 - 31,928 = 58,072

12. 63,764 - 21,548 = 42,216

13. $9605.13 - $2715.96 = $6889.17

14. 76,421 - 73,101 = 3320

15. $8.25 - $6.50 = $1.75

16. (583)(.50) = 291.50

17. (.35)(1045) = 365.75

18. (25)(2513) = 62,825

19. (423)(.01) = 4.23

20. (6.70)(3.2) = 21.44

# TEST 3

DIRECTIONS: Each question or incomplete statement is followed by several suggested answers or completions. Select the one that *BEST* answers the question or completes the statement. *PRINT THE LETTER OF TEE CORRECT ANSWER IN THE SPACE AT THE RIGHT.*

Questions 1-4.

DIRECTIONS: For each of Questions 1-4, perform the indicated arithmetic and choose the correct answer from among the four choices given.

1. 12.485
   + 347

   A. 12,038   B. 12,128   C. 12,782   D. 12,832

   1._____

2. 74,137
   + 711

   A. 74,326   B. 74,848   C. 78,028   D. .D. 78,926

   2._____

3. 3,749
   - 671

   A. 3,078   B. 3,168   C. 4,028   D. 4,420

   3._____

4. 19,805
   -18904

   A. 109   B. 901   C. 1,109   D. 1,901

   4._____

5. When 119 is subtracted from the sum of 2016 + 1634, the remainder is:

   A. 2460   B. 3531   C. 3650   D. 3769

   5._____

6. Multiply 35 X 65 X 15.

   A. 2275   B. 24265   C. 31145   D. 34125

   6._____

7. 90% expressed as a decimal is:

   A. .009   B. .09   C. .9   D. 9.0

   7._____

8. Seven-tenths of a foot expressed in inches is:

   A. 5.5   B. 6.5   C. 7   D. 8.4

   8._____

9. If 95 men were divided into crews of five men each, the *number* of crews that will be formed is:

   A. 16   B. 17   C. 18   D. 19

   9._____

10. If a man earns $19.50 an hour, the *number* of working hours it will take him to earn $4,875 is, most nearly,

    A. 225  B. 250  C. 275  D. 300

11. If 5 1/2 loads of gravel cost $55.00, then 6 1/2 loads will cost:

    A. $60.  B. $62.50  C. $65.  D. $66.00

12. At $2.50 a yard, 27 yards of concrete will cost:

    A. $36.  B. $41.80  C. $54.  D. $67.50

13. A distance is measured and found to be 52.23 feet. In feet and inches, this distance is, most nearly, 52 feet *and*

    A. 2 3/4"  B. 3 1/4"  C. 3 3/4"  D. 4 1/4"

14. If a maintainer gets $5.20 per hour and time and one-half for working over 40 hours, his *gross* salary for a week in which he worked 43 hours would be

    A. $208.00  B. $223.60  C. $231.40  D. $335.40

15. The circumference of a circle is given by the formula $C = \Pi D$, where C is the circumference, D is the diameter, and $\Pi$ is about 3 1/7.
    If a coil is 15 turns of steel cable has an average diameter of 20 inches, the *total* length of cable on the coil is *nearest to*

    A. 5 feet  B. 78 feet  C. 550 feet  D. 943 feet

16. The measurements of a poured concrete foundation show that 54 cubic feet of concrete have been placed.
    If payment for this concrete is to be on the basis of cubic yards, the 54 cubic feet must be

    A. multiplied by 27  B. multiplied by 3
    C. divided by 27     D. divided by 3

17. If the cost of 4 1/2 tons of structural steel is $1,800, then the cost of 12 tons is, most nearly,

    A. $4,800  B. $5,400  C. $7,200  D. $216,000

18. An hourly-paid employee working 12:00 midnight to 8:00 a.m. is directed to report to the medical staff for a physical examination at 11:00 a.m. of the same day.
    The pay allowed him for reporting will be an extra

    A. 1 hour  B. 2 hours  C. 3 hours  D. 4 hours

19. The *total* length of four pieces of 2" pipe, whose lengths are 7' 3 1/2", 4' 2 3/16", 5' 7 5/16", and 8' 5 7/8", respectively, is:

    A. 24' 6 3/4"        B. 24' 7 15/16"
    C. 25' 5 13/16"      D. 25' 6 7/8"

20. As a senior mortuary caretaker, you are preparing a monthly report, using the following figures:  20._____

    No. of bodies received                      983
    No. of bodies claimed                        720
    No. of bodies sent to city cemetery         14
    No. of bodies sent to medical schools       9

How many bodies remained at the end of the monthly reporting period?

    A. 230      B. 240      C. 250      D. 260

## KEY (CORRECT ANSWERS)

| | | | |
|---|---|---|---|
| 1. | D | 11. | C |
| 2. | B | 12. | D |
| 3. | A | 13. | A |
| 4. | B | 14. | C |
| 5. | B | 15. | B |
| 6. | D | 16. | C |
| 7. | C | 17. | A |
| 8. | D | 18. | C |
| 9. | D | 19. | D |
| 10. | B | 20. | B |

## SOLUTIONS TO PROBLEMS

1.  12,485 + 347 = 12,832

2.  74,137 + 711 = 74,848

3.  3749 - 671 = 3078

4.  19,805 - 18,904 = 901

5.  (2016 + 1634) - 119 = 3650 - 119 = 3531

6.  (35)(65)(15) = 34,125

7.  90% = .90 or .9

8.  $(\frac{7}{10})(12) = 8.4$ inches

9.  95 ÷ 5 = 19  crews

10. $4875 ÷ $19.50 = 250 days

11. Let x = cost. Then, $\frac{5\frac{1}{2}}{6\frac{1}{2}} = \frac{\$55.00}{x}$.  $5\frac{1}{2} = 357.50$. Solving, x = $65

12. ($2.50)(27) = $67.50

13. .23-ft. = 2.76 in., so 52.23 ft $\approx$ 52 ft. $2\frac{3}{4}$ in. ($.76 \approx \frac{3}{4}$)

14. Salary = ($5.20)(40) + ($7.80)(3) = $231.40

15. Length $\approx (15)(3\frac{1}{7})(20) \approx 943$ in. $\approx 78$ ft.

16. There are 27 cu.ft. in 1 cu.yd. To change from 54 cu.ft. to cu.yds., divide by 27.

17. $1800 ÷ $4\frac{1}{2}$ = = $400 per ton. Then, 12 tons cost ($400)(12) = $4800

18. Instead of working 12 to 8, he will be staying until 11 AM, an extra 3 hours.

19. $7'3\frac{1}{2}" + 4'2\frac{3}{16}" + 5'7\frac{5}{16}" + 8'5\frac{7}{8}" = 24'17\frac{30}{16}" = 24'18\frac{7}{8}"$

20. 983 - 720 - 14 - 9 = 240 bodies left.

# POLICE SCIENCE NOTES
# DETENTION PROCEDURES

### Introduction

Generally detention is thought of as confinement of a prisoner in a jail facility from his formal booking to his formal release. This includes a period of time when he is merely held for bail or court appearance, when he is held after trial for formal sentencing, and when he is actually serving time in a jail or prison. Actually his arrest restricts or removes his freedom and places him under official restraint; thus, it is at this point that his actual detention begins.

Responsibility for the prisoner before booking may be solely that of the arresting officer or it may be given over to jail personnel assigned to transport him to the detention facility. We are concerned, therefore, as a practical matter with the entire time the prisoner is in official custody beginning with his arrest and ending with his release from custody.

Security is the essence of detention and implies assurance against escape or rescue of the prisoner. It also implies a full measure of personal safety for the officers, the prisoner himself, other inmates and visitors and other citizens.

Although it has been implied, and is true in fact, that our concern is with persons arrested for the commission of crimes, our responsibility is a broader one. The more broad responsibility will be increasingly important in time of natural disaster or civil defense emergency. The latter includes the "holding" for safekeeping of the mentally and physically incompetent, children without parents or who are lost or abandoned, persons who are threatened by mobs or individuals, and those who must be held as material witnesses. While legal and procedural provisions must be made to handle each of the above, this is a local matter not detailed here.

### Transportation

Usually an arresting officer makes a search of his prisoner at the time of arrest for dangerous weapons, means of self-destruction, and less frequently, for evidence of a crime. Officers should be trained and required to make this search. Nonetheless, since it is often made under unusual conditions of stress, transporting and booking officers should also conduct searches with final responsibility lying with the booking officer. Adequate search is a protection to police and jailers, to the prisoner and other inmates, and to visitors and other citizens.

The search, however, only removes one kind of danger; the security measure of adequate restraint must be provided to avoid loss of the prisoner by his own actions or those of others. The restraint is also provided, of course, as another means of preventing injury to the prisoner and to others.

Transportation should be considered as any means used to get the prisoner from one point to another which is usually considered to be from the location of arrest to the place of detention. Transportation, however, is also involved in taking the prisoner to court, in moving him from one place of detention to another, and in taking him to the site of work details or assignments. For our purposes we must assume that transportation may mean moving the prisoner on foot, in a special or regular police automobile, in a special prisoner vehicle (paddywagon or prisoner van) or by other means including aircraft or boats.

The same general precautions apply to all means of transport because the need for security and restraint exists in all. Transport by walking should only be considered in the absence of a proper vehicle, for very short distances, or when physical circumstances may require it, as in moving the prisoner from a detention facility to a court. The number of officers required varies according to apparent need but also according to prescribed regulations. Only one officer is required in the transport of noncriminal nonviolent persons in protective custody and these include children, the aged, minor offenders, and others. Two officers should be used normally for a person under criminal arrest if there is even a nominal possibility of escape or rescue. Three or more officers should be used in serious criminal cases, cases involving a violent prisoner, or where there is likely to be a serious attempt to escape, rescue, or attack the prisoner.

Two officers should almost always be used in prisoner transport by vehicle except in minor cases when the prisoner is placed in a separate, secure and specially designed section of the vehicle screened off from the driver. When a vehicle is used all doors should be locked and inside handles removed from the prisoner section, as in the rear of an automobile.

Minimal restraint is required when the prisoner is in a secure and separate section of the vehicle unless conflict among prisoners may develop. Reasonable restraint should be used otherwise and will usually involve the use of handcuffs. Whenever handcuffs and other restraining devices are required public display of their use should be avoided.

Special precautions should be used at the place of detention because this is the most likely point of escape or rescue. It is important that detention officers assist transporting officers in placing prisoners in the detention facility. Although the prisoner has been under restraint since his arrest, detention in a formal sense begins when he is placed in the detention facility. Properly booking and admitting the prisoner is of utmost importance and carefully prescribed admittance procedures should be established and followed. The latter, of course, must conform to State and local legal requirements. A prisoner's property, and evidence also, must be properly identified, receipted, and secured. Identification of property should be witnessed under most circumstances and especially when the prisoner is unable to sign for it. Securing property implies controlling it so that it may be returned intact on the prisoner's release.

Fingerprinting and photographing of each prisoner should be required in all criminal cases and in emergency conditions where accurate identification is important as when the prisoner is suffering from amnesia. Exceptions to this practice may be established, i.e., if the prisoner had been previously arrested and his identification established prior to the present arrest.

A final detailed and complete search must be made. The search should be for evidence if this is appropriate under the circumstances; however, the principal purpose at this point is probably to remove offensive weapons and means of self-destruction. Before a prisoner is placed in a cell it should be carefully searched also.

Capabilities for medical examination of incoming prisoners, especially those who are sick or injured, should be provided. This is not only humane but may prevent serious problems later including criticism for failure to provide proper care. Under some circumstances a detailed medical examination for all prisoners may be practicable. In this case, by formal regulation, prisoners falling in certain categories must be examined. Categories should include any person over 60 years of age as this age group will usually contain a much higher percentage of persons requiring care than would those who are younger; any person with a history of illness or disability known to the officers by prior acquaintance with the person or through medical records he carries on his person; any person who is apparently, although not necessarily obviously, ill or injured; any prisoner who complains of illness or injury; and any person who is unconscious or comatose.

It is standard practice in detention facilities to provide for separation of prisoners by age and sex. Quite obviously juveniles and adults should not be quartered together, nor should men be placed with women. Those who have communicable diseases or who may have been exposed to them should be placed in quarantine sections. Those who are perverts or who exhibit tendencies to perversion should be separated from others, particularly children. Those who are mentally deranged, or who apparently become so, must also be isolated. This may be an especially important consideration under emer-gency conditions. Less serious offenders should be separated from the more serious offenders to avoid recruiting prisoners to the ranks of major criminals. The use of psychiatrists and medical personnel is recommended to assist in determining necessary separation in the case of perversion and mental derangement.

Providing adequate security is essential. All offensive weapons and means of self-destruction must be physically protected and adequately guarded. None should be within reach of any prisoner. Guards should not carry firearms while in any prisoner section. Full control of all means of entrance and exit must be provided. No guard should have on his person a set of keys which would allow escape from or admittance to the full facility or a series of its sections. All tools require close control because they may be used as weapons, escape devices, or provide the means to make such items. Prisoners being returned to cells from corridors, shops, and dining rooms should be searched.

Medical supplies must be carefully controlled. Their possession by prisoners provide means of self-destruction and barter. Under some circumstances prisoners would maliciously destroy essential medical provisions.

On a frequent, intermittent basis, quarters and inmates must be inspected and prisoners counted.

To avoid emotional problems, provide exercise, and for other reasons prisoners who warrant the trust can be given some freedom in the facility and be put to minor but productive tasks. Classification of prisoners as "trusties" or available for light work must be carefully done to avoid escapes and other problems.

All security measures must be established on a basis that allows prompt implementation of plans for evacuation of prisoners in the event of fire or facility destruction by other means. Planning must also provide full means of protection against the consequences of riot and mob attempts at rescue or attack. This may require provisions to quickly and inconspicuously move key prisoners to other detention.

## Detention When Jails Unavailable

Most shelters and relocation facilities are not designed for detention purposes. This will require imaginative improvisation of both quarters and procedures. Two things must be provided in spite of adverse circumstances: (1) Basic security for prisoners, officers, and other occupants; and (2) separation of various categories of prisoners.

Large rooms, of course, can be used for group detention if adequate security is provided and if the need for separation is minimal or absent. Such use of space, however, may require the use of additional guards constantly on the alert to avoid altercations or plotting for escape.

In shelters the problems of security and separation may require unusual use of restraining devices and materials. Individual prisoners can be handcuffed to pipes, doorknobs, stanchions, or window bars. If this is done, adequate free space around the prisoner should be provided to avoid improper and dangerous contact with other prisoners or occupants of the shelter. Two prisoners can be secured with a single set of handcuffs merely by passing the cuffs behind a pipe set close to a wall or the floor, or behind a bar in a barred window or door.

Ropes, belts, and similar material may be used in lieu of handcuffs, but require unusual care to avoid injury or escapes. Although it may be necessary to occasionally check handcuffs to see that they are not too tight for the comfort or safety of the prisoner, frequent inspection of rope and other nonmetallic material is essential. These may quickly become either too tight and thus cause injury, or too loose and thus permit escape. Restraints of material must also be checked if they become wet, or dry out after being wet.

Sedatives may be used under unusual circumstances by a doctor or by a nurse under his direction. Sedatives have a particular value when handling a violent person and may be used both as a restraint and treatment in many cases.

Expensive, but necessary on occasion, will be the use of guards or officers on the basis of one guard to a prisoner. This should be avoided if possible because of the excessive drain it puts on available personnel.

## Conclusion

It should be said once again that security is the essence of detention. The safety of officers, prisoners, and others is dependent on strict adherence to carefully prepared procedures.

# POLICE SCIENCE NOTES

## COLLECTION, IDENTIFICATION AND PRESERVATION OF EVIDENCE

The Definition and importance of Evidence

### Definition

Evidence can be defined as "any medium of proof or probative matter, legally presented at the trial of any issue, by the participants of the trial and through the medium of witnesses, records, documents, objects, etc., for the purpose of inducing belief in the minds of the court and the jurors as to its creditability and contention." In more general terms, evidence is anything that can be legally presented to indicate the guilt of a criminal act or to aid in determining the truth about any fact in question.

### Importance

The primary importance of evidence is the aid it offers in the identification of the guilty party and in his successful prosecution. Because of this, the proper collection, identification, and preservation of evidence make up a vital part of police operations. Cases may be won or lost depending upon the proficiency of the police department in this area.

Evidence is the means by which the patrolman or investigator can aid the prosecutor in giving the court a complete picture of the crime and its commission. It explains the facts that the officer uses to determine that the accused is guilty. Properly prepared and presented, evidence may serve the same purpose as taking the court and the jury to the scene of the crime and reconstructing the events which led to the commission of the crime charged.

In order to insure that this vital function is performed properly, most departments have specialists known as criminal investigators to collect, search and properly evaluate evidence. The reason for this is that such specialization saves time and leaves the patrolman free to resume his primary duties once the investigator arrives at the scene. However, since the general patrolman or the auxiliary policeman will usually be the first to arrive at the scene and therefore is crucial to the outcome of the criminal investigation, it is important that they have an adequate understanding of evidence and be skilled in its preservation and protection. The need for developing adequate investigative skills is especially crucial in those departments without a specialist and where the officers are expected to conduct their own investigation.

### Classification of Evidence

Evidence may be divided into three major classifications:

*DIRECT evidence* directly establishes the main fact of issue. It applies immediately to the fact to be proven or disproven and is usually what a person sees, hears, or knows.

*CIRCUMSTANTIAL evidence* tends to prove or disprove the fact in issue by other facts leading to a presumption of the truth or falsity of the main fact. The essence here is inference-establishing a factor or circumstance from which a court may infer another fact. It may be real evidence or things which may be said to "speak for themselves." Ownership of the murder weapon, the fingerprints thereon, and the inability of the accused to account for his actions at the time of the crime would be matters of circumstantial evidence.

*REAL OR PHYSICAL evidence* comprises those tangible objects introduced at the trial which speak for themselves and need no explanation, just identification. Examples of real evidence would be guns, fingerprints, and bloodstains. Real evidence can be further divided into:

*FIXED OR IMMOVABLE evidence* which by its very nature cannot be moved from the crime scene. It includes such objects as latent fingerprints, tool marks, doors, windows, wall plaster, etc. Of course, fingerprints may be lifted, casts made of foot and tire marks, and photographs taken of the entire scene; but the actual object remains incapable of being transported to the courtroom.

*MOVABLE evidence* which can be preserved intact for examination at headquarters and presentation in the courtroom. This includes such objects as bullets, tools, hair, documents, clothing, and many other similar objects.

### Chain of Custody - The Cardinal Rule of Evidence

In order for the evidence to be properly admitted into court, its location and holder must be accurately established from the time the officer or investigator finds the evidence until it is presented in court. If the whereabouts of the evidence cannot be established, even for a moment, the court will rule it is inadmissible. The reason for this is because if it can be shown that the evidence was out of responsible hands or unaccountable for, then it is also likely that the evidence could have been tampered with thereby negating its validity and leaving the court no alternative but to dismiss it. Therefore, in order to overcome the questions presented by the defense and to impress the judge and jury that the evidence has been properly protected, the police officer must establish an accurate "chain of custody" for each piece of evidence presented in court.

Perhaps the best method of maintaining an accurate chain of custody is through the use of receipts. If the evidence is to be out of the officer's hand for even a minute he should demand a receipt containing: the time, date, and place where the exchange occurred, to whom the evidence was given, and for what purpose. Likewise, if the officer receives any evidence for transportation or for other purposes he should fill out and give a receipt to the person giving him the evidence.

### Collection of Evidence

Two points to be remembered by all personnel concerned with the collection of evidence are: (1) there, is rarely a major crime committed without some kind of evidence being left at the scene, and (2) nothing at a crime scene is too significant to be overlooked. The ultimate success of any investigation will depend on the acumen of the officers in searching the scene, recognizing evidence, and preserving it.

### Preliminary Activities at the Crime Scene

The first officer at the crime scene who will usually be either the beat patrolman or the auxiliary policeman should:
1. Assist the injured when necessary.
2. Notify the proper experts and equipment to conduct a proper crime scene examination.
3. Obtain pertinent data from the witnesses and any suspects, keeping them separated if possible.
4. Use the most effective means possible to protect the crime scene from any intrusions by unauthorized personnel.
5. Arrest any perpetrators caught at or near the scene.
6. Assist the investigator when he arrives to examine the scene.

The investigator or whoever is in charge of the investigation should determine from the initial officer what has been done and what needs to be done before taking command of the situation. He will then conduct a thorough investigation of the scene and question all witnesses, victims, and suspects at the scene.

**Examination of the Crime Scene**

Usually the first person to be admitted to the crime scene is the photographer who will take as many photographs as necessary to insure proper coverage of the scene for further study and analysis. While the photographer is shooting the scene, the investigator will make a sketch of the scene to supplement the photographs by adding the dimensions of height, distances, and locations of the scene. Notes should also be made of the camera's position, characteristics, and the weather conditions that affect the camera's settings.

The next step in the process is the search of the crime scene area which presents various problems, especially when the area is extensive. It is essential that proper consideration be given to all aspects of the search problems before proceeding, in order that the search can be made as complete and as thorough as possible. The general organization of the search party will be determined by the size and type of the area to be covered, available personnel, and the equipment with which the party must work. It is important that the search party be divided into manageable units with each unit aware of just what area it is responsible for searching.

The number of men necessary to conduct a search will largely depends on the conditions existing at the time. Search parties may consist of as many as a hundred men, but should never be less than two. Regardless of how many people conduct the search, a careful and methodical effort must be exerted, the search should proceed according to plan, and the searchers should search for one thing at a time. If the search is going to be for fingerprints then the search should be for fingerprints only until they are all found or there is good reason to believe that there are none. Then the search can be for bloodstains or hair, and so on down the line. The searchers may note the presence and location of one piece of evidence while looking for another piece, but the evidence noted should not be touched until the searchers are specifically looking for it. It is also a good practice to have each man responsible for a particular duty during the search. He can be a note taker, sketcher, evidence collector, or whatever else is necessary. Then when the search starts again he should be switched to another duty. This helps keep the persons alert, and insure adequate coverage of the scene. Never search a crime scene just once; always go over and over the scene until everyone is satisfied that all the evidence has been found. However, do not handle evidence more than is necessary.

**The Identification of Evidence**

To insure the proper chain of custody of any evidence found during the search it is necessary that every piece of evidence be marked for identification by the person who found it. Others who witness its finding should also mark the evidence of witness. If the evidence does not provide sufficient suitable area for more than a single mark it should be marked by the finding officer and witnessed by other persons. The characteristics of the mark should be recorded in the notes of the officer as well as the witnesses.

The following steps should be followed in the marking of any evidence:

1. Each bit of evidence should be appropriately marked at the time it is removed from its original position. No piece of evidence should be removed from the position in which it was found until after it has been photographed, sketched, processed for latent fingerprints, and listed in the investigator's notebook.

2. The mark "X" should never be used to identify evidence. The identifying mark should be one that is characteristic and easily identifiable. Using the written initials of the finder is considered best. The mark used and its position as well as any serial numbers or distinctive marks present on the object should be recorded in the officer's notebook for further reference.

3. Whenever possible mark the object itself, taking extreme care to prevent any destruction of the value of the evidence. Unless evidence or the article itself prohibits it, the marks made on all articles of a similar nature should be in the same direction.

4. Always mark the container in which the object is being placed as well as the object. If the object cannot be marked then seal the container and mark the seal as well as the container.

Proper marking and the keeping of notes on the evidence found during the course of an investigation will make it possible for the officer to positively identify each piece of evidence at the time it is presented in court. Using a mark which is characteristic and one that will not have been accidentally placed on the evidence, as well as knowing just where to locate the mark on the evidence is of great value to the officer witness. He will be poised and confident in his manner of handling the evidence and the judge and jury will be more impressed as to the value of the evidence presented.

**Preservation and transportation of Evidence Preservation**

Each article of evidence should be placed in an appropriate container depending on the nature and size of the evidence. It is recommended that the container used should be larger than necessary to normally accommodate the evidence article, so as to prevent it from being crushed or squeezed by other articles. However, the container should not be so large as to cause damage to the evidence from excessive movement. The containers should be new and clean and each article of evidence should be packed in a separate container. This is especially necessary where evidence might have foreign matter adhering to it. Should any matter adhering to the evidence fall or become separated from the article during or after packing, it will be found in the container in which the article was packed.

**Transporting the Article**

The transportation of the sealed evidence to the laboratory should be accompanied by the officer who collected the evidence. It has to be shipped to a laboratory, the safest and most practical method of delivery should be used and in the case of perishables, the speediest method possible should be employed.

The contents of any container should be clearly listed on the package or label. If several individual packages are packed into a single large container, the larger container should be labeled to show the content of the individual containers. This would be in addition to the labels on the individual containers. The information contained on the package should include: (1) contents of the package, (2) name of the person from whom the property was taken or where it was found, (3) the number of the case on which the evidence has a bearing, (4) the date and time it was found, (5) the name of the officer who found or received it and (6) the article to be subjected to laboratory examination, and (7) the type of examination suggested.

## Storage of Evidence

One of the most important phases of maintaining the value of the evidence is its storage. The evidence must be stored in such a manner that there is no question as to actual possession.

In some departments the officer has to store the evidence in his personal locker, in others, special wall lockers are set aside for the storage of evidence with keys only available to the officer in charge of each watch and the officer who has evidence to store.

Probably the best arrangement would be for the department to have a property room with an officer from each watch in charge. After obtaining evidence the officer could then place it in the property room and receive a receipt for it. This room should have the proper facilities for storing evidence along with a strict security apparatus to keep all people except the officer of each watch in charge of it from entering.

This way the evidence could be properly stored according to its needs and the officer can be assured that the evidence has been under strict control and carefully guarded until it is needed in the laboratory or in the courtroom. He can then maintain the chain of evidence and assure the court and jury the evidence was given the best of care and handled by responsible personnel.

## Conclusion

The identification, collection, and preservation of evidence are of crucial importance to the execution of police responsibilities. The auxiliary policeman will be expected to take part in these duties when the occasion arises. His specific duties will naturally depend upon the department with which he is allied. However, in most departments because of the presence of specialists in the area of criminal investigation his main duties will be the protection of the scene and assisting the specialists where necessary. Regardless of what his duties are, the auxiliary policeman should constantly strive to gain further knowledge about this field for his own benefit. In a natural or manmade disaster he may be the only representative of the law left within an entire area and, at that time, his knowledge of proper investigative techniques will help continue law and order in society.

The auxiliary officer should remember that there are always clues at a crime scene and that everything within a crime scene is significant. Only knowledge, experience, and patience will bring these clues into the open and these take time to develop. He should never forget the importance of maintaining the chain of custody by issuing and receiving receipts. Above all, he should be constantly aware of the importance of evidence and should constantly try to improve his own skills in its identification, collection, and preservation.

# BASIC FUNDAMENTALS OF FINGERPRINT SCIENCE

## I. IMPORTANCE OF FINGERPRINTS AS PHYSICAL EVIDENCE

Fingerprints are perhaps the most common form of physical evidence, and certainly one of the most valuable. They relate directly to the ultimate objective of every criminal investigation--the identification of the offender.

Fingerprints of the offender are frequently found at the scene of a crime, and they may take more than one form. However, in all cases, the prints are fragile and susceptible to complete destruction by the first careless act. They are also, in many cases, difficult to find. This chapter discusses the basic requirements for conducting a successful search for fingerprints, together with the means of recognizing, lifting, and preserving them for later analysis.

With but a few exceptions, everyone has fingerprints. This universal character is a prime factor in the establishment of a standard of identification. Since a print of one finger has never been known to exactly duplicate another fingerprint (even of the same person or identical twin) it is possible to identify an individual with just one impression. The relative ease with which a set of inked fingerprints can be taken as a means of identifcation is a further basis for using this standard. Despite such factors as aging and a variety of environmental influences, a person's fingerprints have never been known to change. The unchanging pattern thus provides a permanent record of the individual throughout life.

Although there are many different filing systems for fingerprints, each is based on classification of common characteristics. The classification system works to readily categorize a set of fingerprints, as well as to provide quick access to a set of prints with a given characteristic.

## II. DEFINITION OF FINGERPRINTS

A direct or inked fingerprint is an impression of the ridge detail of the underside of the fingers, palms, toes, or the soles of the feet. This is contrasted with a latent print, which is an impression caused by the perspiration through the sweat pores on the ridges of the skin being transferred to some surface. Fingerprints also occur as residues when the finger ridges have been contaminated with such materials as oil, dirt, blood, and grease.

## III. BASIS OF IDENTIFICATION OF FINGERPRINTS

The ridge detail of fingerprints including ends of ridges, their separations, and their relationship to each other constitute the basis for identification of fingerprints. The basic points of comparison of prints are shown in Figure 1. In checking for similarity, most experts require from 10 to 12 points although there is no specific number required. However, regardless of the points of similarity, should an unexplainable difference appear, positive identification cannot be made.

There is no set print size requirement for positive identification. The only requirement is that the print be large enough to contain at least 10 to 12 points. This requirement count may be met by an area as small as the end of a pencil. As a general rule, if the investigator develops an area which appears to have several ridges, regardless of the size of the area, it should be lifted, marked, and submitted to the laboratory.

Some investigators believe that the points used for identification of the fingerprint occur only in the pattern area of the finger. This is not true. All the different types occur outside of the pattern area on the finger as well as on the first and second joint of the finger and the entire palm of the hand. They are also present on the toes and the entire sole of the foot. In fact, they may be found in any area where friction ridges occur.

## IV. LIMITATIONS OF LATENT PRINTS

Even though latent prints are invaluable in the course of investigative work, there are certain limitations as to what information these prints can be expected to provide. It is impossible, for example, to determine the age of the latent print because there are a number of factors other than time that change the appearance of the developed latent. It is sometimes possible, however, to estimate the age of the print in relation to certain events. For example, prints appearing on an object thoroughly cleaned during a recent housecleaning can be dated as occurring after that event.

Likewise, it is not possible to determine, from the examination of the print alone, the age or sex of the person leaving the print. Even though a rough correlation does exist between age and sex and such characteristics as size of the ridge or pattern, individual variations occur.

## BASIC FINGERPRINT COMPARISONS

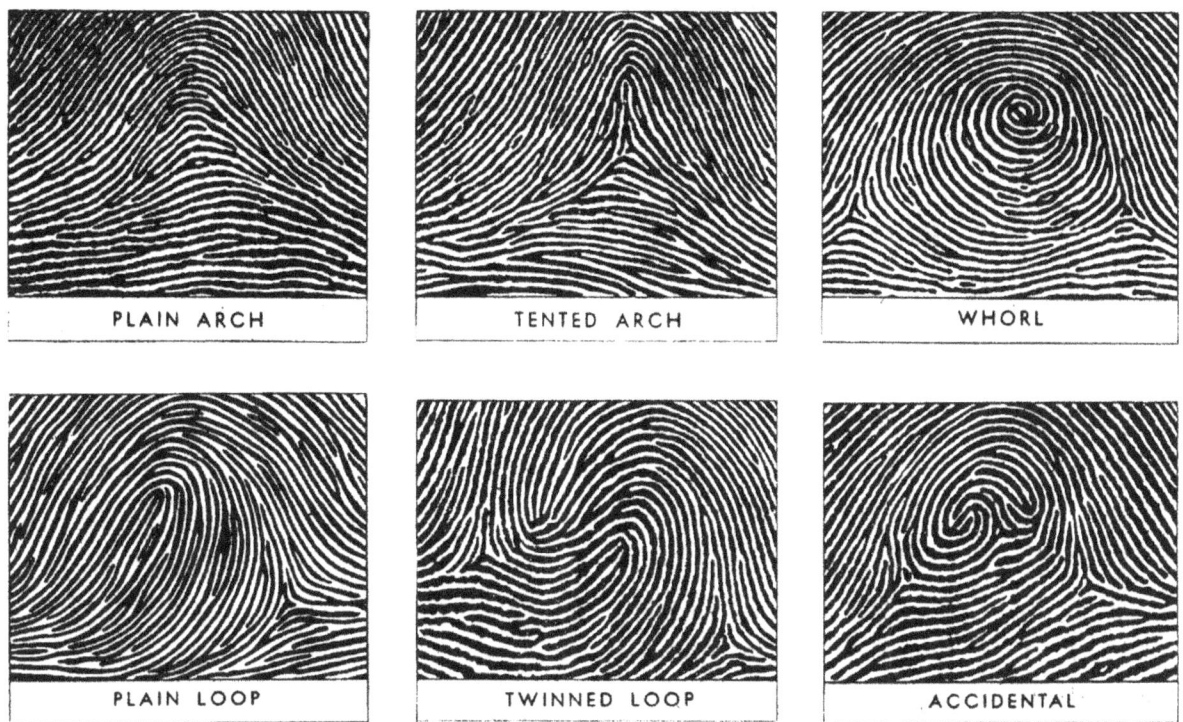

FIGURE 1

Prints cannot be used to identify the race of a suspect, nor can occupational groups be determined with an accepted degree of accuracy on the basis of fingerprints. It is true that many occupations, such as bricklaying, cause certain characteristic damage to the skin of the fingers and hands. However, any conjecture as to occupation of a suspect made on this basis should be considered only as an investigative lead and not as substantive evidence.

## V.  CONDITIONS WHICH AFFECT LATENT PRINTS

The quality of latent fingerprints is affected by such conditions as the type of surface material, the manner in which the print was transferred, nature and quantity of the substance (perspiration, oils, blood, etc.) which covered the ridge surfaces, weather conditions, and, to some extent, the physical or occupational defects of the person transferring the print. The processing of prints as it relates to these conditions is discussed later under "METHOD OF DEVELOPING FINGERPRINTS."

The nature and the condition of the surface on which the latent print is deposited are very important. The surface must be fairly clean and smooth or the ridge detail of the finger will be lost. Such surfaces as coarse cloth, unfinished wood, grained leather, etc., are very poor surfaces for fingerprints.

Another important consideration is the manner in which the object was touched or released. The ridges on fingers are very close together. Should the finger move just the distance between two ridges when touching or releasing an object, most of the ridge detail will be lost. This condition explains why most latents which are developed are smeared in the pattern area and only their ridges outside the pattern area have enough detail for identification.

There are conditions which occur that cause the friction surfaces to become completely covered with perspiration or other materials. When such materials cover not only the ridge surface of the skin, but fill the valleys as well, no ridge detail can be recorded. Prints of this type generally develop very dark and appear about the same as a print that was developed with too much powder.

The weather affects the latent print in a number of ways. The print may be dried out or washed away. Humidity will cause latent prints on paper to become smudged or even disappear. Because of the sponge nature of paper, moisture enters it from all directions and causes the ridge detail to diffuse to the extent that it will not be recognized as a print.

The more oil that is deposited with perspiration, the longer the print will last. Since perspiration is mostly water, the oil that is deposited with it will float on the surface and reduce its evaporation rate. After the water evaporates, the oil remains and becomes quite tacky. This condition results in better development of the ridge detail when using fingerprint powder. Body oil is present on the friction ridges of the fingers as contamination from the hairy parts of the body and, therefore, may not be present in the latent print at all. When no oils are present, the water content of the deposited material is subject to the same evaporation rate as any like amount of water under the same conditions and the print will be less tacky.

## VI. RESPONSIBILITY OF THE CRIME SCENE INVESTIGATOR IN COLLECTING FINGERPRINTS

Latent prints are such valuable evidence that extraordinary efforts should be made to recover them. The investigator is strongly urged to adopt a positive attitude toward this aspect of the search, regardless of any apparent problems.

It is absolutely imperative that the crime scene investigator make a thorough search of all surface areas in and around the scene of the crime that have the potential of retaining finger or palm prints. Particular attention should be paid to the less obvious places, such as the undersides of tiolet seats, table tops and dresser drawers, the surface of dinner plates, filing cabinets, the backs of chairs, rearview mirrors (both the glass and frame) and the trunk lids of automobiles. Heavily handled objects, such as door knobs or telephones, may not yield good prints. However, they are objects that are quite likely to be touched and should always be processed.

The investigator should not assume that the offender took precautions against leaving prints or that he destroyed those he did leave. A person committing a criminal offense is usually under some stress and may be prone to oversight. If he wore gloves he may have removed them for some operation, or they may have been torn.

It is helpful to attempt to view the scene as the criminal did. Hence, such conditions as time of day, weather, and physical layout may suggest that certain surface areas should be closely examined. In conducting the examination for latent prints in a burglary case, for example, it is suggested that the investigation begin at the point of entry. For other crimes, such as rape, the point of entry takes on less importance as a source of latent prints. Whatever the nature of the crime and the particular circumstances, its reconstruction by the investigator is intended to give practical direction to the search.

Valuable aid in obtaining latent print leads may be solicited from a person who is familiar with the usual physical layout of the crime scene, such as the owner of the building or the usual occupant of an apartment. That person should be allowed to observe at least a part of the preliminary investigation and be encouraged to point out items which appear out of place or to identify objects that may have been brought in by the suspect.

Things which have permanent serial numbers attached to them, such as automobiles, weapons, and machinery require special attention. In addition to checking such items for latent prints, it is good policy to make a lift of the serial number (using fingerprint tape), as well as prints and attach both to the same fingerprint card. Such direct lifts of serial numbers prove invaluable for latter reference, particularly as evidence in court.

## VII. PRINTS WHICH REQUIRE NO FURTHER DEVELOPING

There are two basic types of latent prints that the crime scene examiner will likely encounter which do not need developing. The first of these is the visible type created after the suspect's hand has come in contact with blood, ink, paint, grease, dirt, etc., and the print transferred to some surface area. Prints made from these substances are usually distinct and should stand out to the investigator. The procedure to be used in collecting the print is to first photograph and then cover it with protective tape. The surface on which the print rests must then be transported to the crime laboratory. Common sense must rule the decision as to just how much damage is justifiable in collecting items or surface areas where prints are found.

The second type of print which requires no further developing is an impression in a soft substance such as putty, clay, or fresh paint. Again, the procedure is to first photograph the impression, then transport the object or a section containing it to the crime laboratory. If a physical transfer of the impression is not possible, it should be sprayed with shellac and a cast prepared of silicone rubber. The cast should then be identified and sent to the laboratory in place of the actual imprint.

## VIII. METHOD OF DEVELOPING FINGERPRINTS

The types of surfaces from which latent prints can be lifted fall into two broad categories: those which are hard, smooth, and nonabsorbent, and those which are smooth and absorbent. The crime scene investigator must be able to distinguish between these two types of surfaces because different procedures are used to develop latent prints on them.

Before developing the print, the fingerprint brush should be cleaned and the bristles separated. This is best done by rolling the handle rapidly between the palms of the hands and letting the bristles spread out naturally.

When the fingerprint powder is stored it tends to compact and becomes difficult to handle. Before opening the container it should be turned upside down and shaken vigorously to loosen the powder.

To determine in which category a given surface belongs, it is useful to think of what would happen to a drop of water if it were placed on it. If the water would bead up (as for example on plate glass) the surface is hard, smooth, and nonabsorbent. However, if the water would soak in, as on cardboard, the surface is absorbent.

IX. <u>Developing Prints on Nonabsorbent, Hard, Smooth Surfaces</u>

Prints made on nonabsorbent, hard materials will remain entirely on the surface of the object in the form of a delicate liquid or semisolid deposit. The print, mainly consisting of oil and water, expands upward from the surface which makes an ideal adhesive base for fingerprint powder.

The actual development process (illustrated in Figure 2) is begun by applying a small amount of fingerprint powder to the area to be examined, using the brush provided in the fingerprint kit. <u>A word of caution: too much powder should not be used since an excessive amount will result in an overly darkened print</u> in which points will be difficult to identify. The brush should just touch the powder, it is not necessary to bury it. The entire area to be processed should be covered using light, even strokes until some ridge detail begins to show. As the pattern of the ridges becomes visible the brush strokes should be directed to follow the contour lines. After all of the details of the print have been developed, the excess powder should be removed by gently brushing or blowing it away. The powder should be allowed to adhere to the wet, tacky area of the latent print but not to the surface on which the print is deposited. The print can be lifted by holding the folded or loose end of the tape with the thumb and the forefinger of one hand and the roll in the other, pulling out enough tape to cover the area to be lifted (usually about 5 or 6 inches), securing the loose end of the tape beside the print to be lifted and holding it there with the forefinger. Then the thumb should slide along the top of the tape forcing it gently down over the print. The roll, which is in the other hand, should not be released during this operation. The print is now protected. The powder used to develop the print is trapped between the tape and the surface of the object. Using care, the tape should be smoothed down over the print to force out all the air bubbles.

Once the tape has been secured, one of two procedures may be followed. If the surface would be destroyed by removing the tape, the tape may be left on and the entire object submitted to the laboratory for examination. If this is not practical, the print may be removed by pulling up on the roll end. When the tape is free of the surface, it is placed on a fingerprint card in the same manner as the tape was placed over the latent print. When the lift is secured to the card, the tape should be severed from the roll and the loose end folded up.

If the developed latent print is larger than the width of the tape, it still may be lifted by placing one strip beside another, allowing about 1/4 inch overlap with each additional strip until the desired area is covered.

## METHOD OF DEVELOPING AND LIFTING LATENT FINGERPRINTS

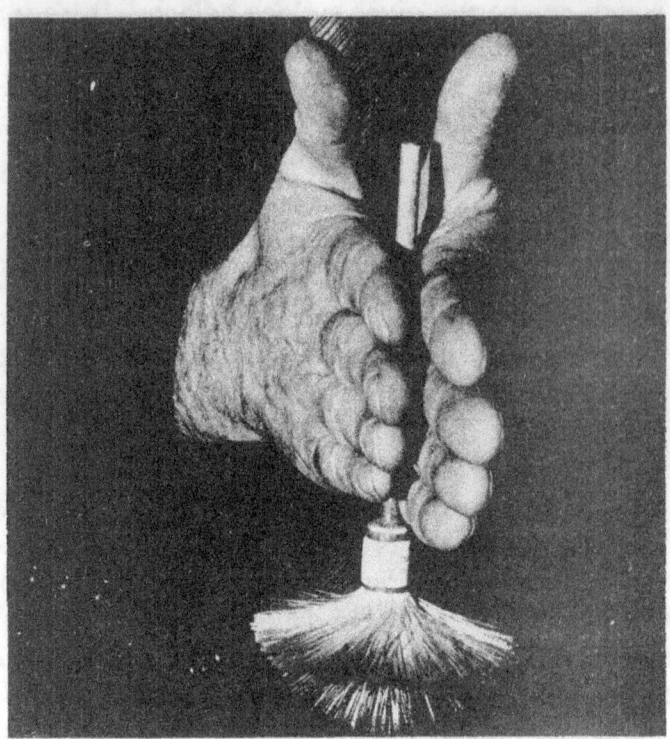

**Fingerprint** brush should be cleaned and bristles separated by rolling **the brush handle rapidly between** the hands.

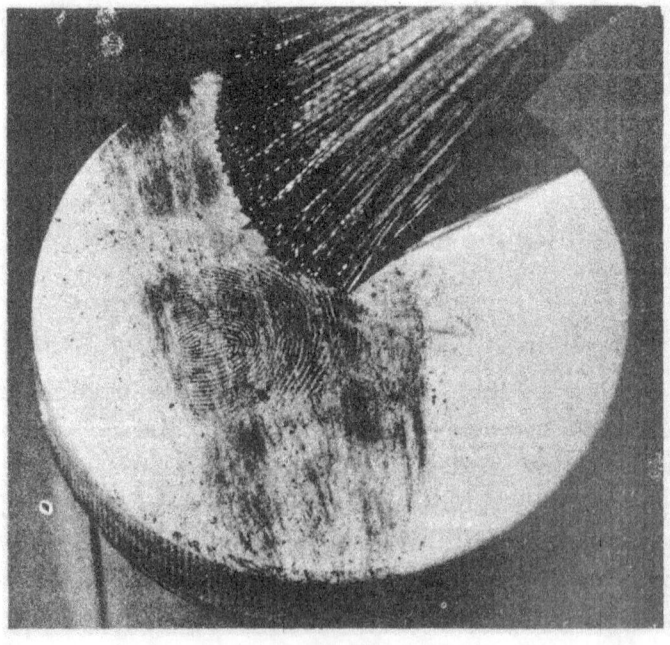

Applying powder to surface to discover the print.

FIGURE 2

# METHOD OF DEVELOPING AND LIFTING LATENT FINGERPRINTS
(Continued)

Cleaning up the print by gently brushing with the flow of the ridges.

Proper method of starting to apply fingerprint tape.

FIGURE 2 (Continued)

## METHOD OF DEVELOPING AND LIFTING LATENT FINGERPRINTS
(Concluded)

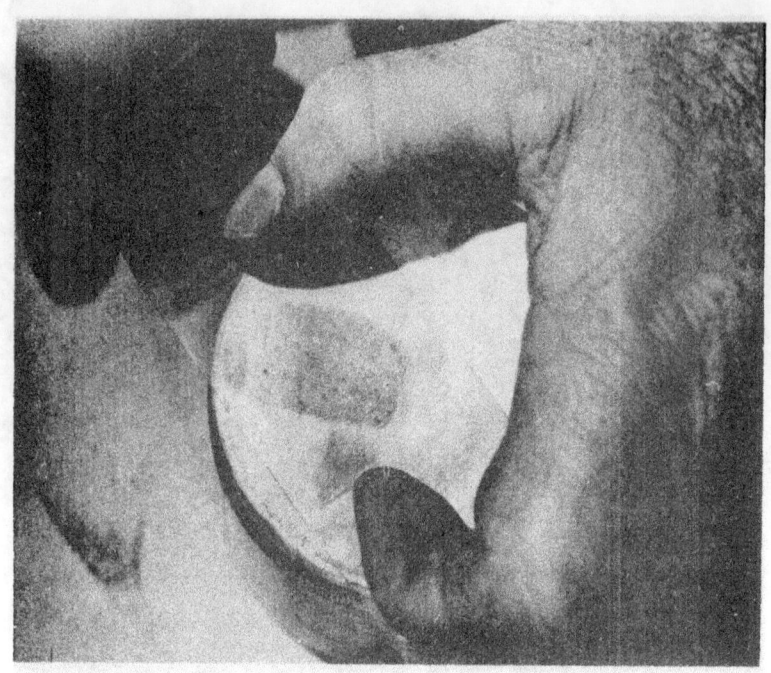

Tape is smoothed with thumb to remove air bubbles.

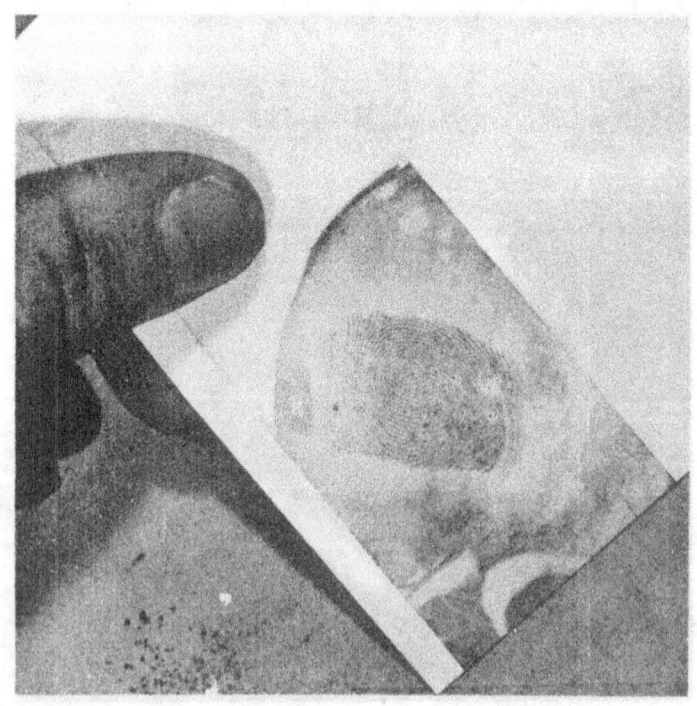

Lifted print is transferred to a fingerprint card.

FIGURE 2 (Concluded)

## X. MARKING AND IDENTIFYING FINGERPRINT LIFTS

After a latent print has been developed, lifted, and placed on a card, it is necessary that the card be properly identified. Information recorded on the card should include the date, title of the case or number, address of the crime scene, name of the officer who made the lift, the exact place of the lift, and the type of object. If the card contains only one lift, the description of the exact place and the type of object lifted from may be placed on the back. If the card contains several lifts (which is permissible), then the exact place and the type object should be written on the front of the card close to the print. Regardless of how well the latent was developed and lifted, if the card is not properly marked with all the information legally required, and if the fingerprint specialist is not furnished with all the information and detail he requires, the whole effort is a waste of time.

In describing the exact place that the lift was made, it is sometimes convenient to draw a simple sketch of the object. This sketch should be made on the fingerprint card which is sent to the criminalistics laboratory. The inclusion of corresponding small arrows on both the lift and the sketch are also helpful in orienting the exact placement of a latent fingerprint.

If prints opposed to each other are lifted, as on both sides of a piece of broken glass, a notation of this fact should be made on the fingerprint card.

## XI. COLLECTION OF ELIMINATION FINGERPRINTS

Before submitting lifted latent prints recovered from the crime scene to a fingerprint technician for examination, elimination prints of all persons who may have had access to the area should be made. With elimination prints, it is possible to exclude from the prints lifted all persons who had legal access to the crime scene.

Equipped with fingerprint ink, a glass plate, and a card holder, the investigator uses the following step-by-step procedure to obtain elimination fingerprints.

- The subject signs the fingerprint card.
- The officer signs and dates the same card.
- The subject washes his hands.
- The officer rolls ink over the surface of the inking slab.
- The officer instructs the subject to relax arm and hand muscles.
- The officer grasps the subject's hand, holds the four fingers back, and inks the thumb by rolling it toward the body. He immediately rolls the inked thumb in the designated space on the card and repeats the process for each of the fingers, rolling them away from the subject's body.

- To make simultaneous impressions, the prints are not rolled; rather the four fingers, extended and joined, are inked and the print is made by exerting a straight down pressure. The process is repeated for the thumbs (again no rolling).
- To make palm prints (needed only if palm prints were found at the crime scene), the entire palm and fingers are inked. The hand is then pressed straight down on a sequence card. A different card should be used for each hand.

If the glass plate and card holder are not available, the ink pad and the elimination cards furnished with the equipment may be used. In case of a homicide, the prints of the victim, including palm prints, must be obtained. The law requires positive identification of all murder victims. Both palm and finger prints are required as elimination prints.

If the investigating officer wishes to take elimination prints, and the equipment for taking inked prints is not available, he may use the same equipment he uses for developing latent prints. The subject's fingers are rolled on a card as though they were inked. After the card has been allowed to dry for a few minutes, the latent prints are dusted with fingerprint powder and when fully developed are covered with fingerprint tape. Both the subject and the officer should sign under a notation on the dated card that the prints are elimination prints.